Economic Development and Political Reform

Economic Development and Political Reform

The Impact of External Capital on the Middle East

Bradley Louis Glasser

Brooklyn College, City University of New York, USA

Edward Elgar

Cheltenham, UK • Northampton MA, USA

Published by
Edward Elgar Publishing Limited
Glensanda House
Montpellier Parade
Cheltenham
Glos GL50 1UA
UK

Edward Elgar Publishing, Inc.
136 West Street
Suite 202
Northampton
Massachusetts 01060
USA

Printed and bound in Great Britain by Bookcraft (Bath) Ltd.

A catalogue record for this book
is available from the British Library

Library of Congress Cataloguing in Publication Data

Glasser, Bradley Louis, 1966–
    Economic development and political reform : impact of external capital on the Middle East / by Bradley Louis Glasser.
    Includes bibliographical references and index.
    1. Middle East—Economic conditions—1979–2. Middle East—Politics and government—1979– I. Title.

HC415.15.G58 2001
338.956'009'048—dc21   00-056006

ISBN 1 85898 927 2

Contents

Acknowledgments

This book grew out of my doctoral research at Columbia University, where I was privileged to work with outstanding students and faculty. Lisa Anderson, F. Gregory Gause III, Douglas Chalmers, Vahid Noshirvani, and Richard Bulliet were members of my demanding and inspiring doctoral committee. I received wonderful intellectual and emotional support from Imco Brouwer, Bryan Daves, Jeremy Foltz, Martin Malin, Robert Nadelson, Chris Toensing, Marc Sable, Vickie Langhor, Lisa Pollard, and Jennifer Rich. The Political Science Department of Columbia University, the Social Science Research Council, and the European University Institute proffered critical financial and institutional assistance. I am particularly indebted to the administrators and fellows of the Mediterranean Program and the Robert Schuman Center of the European University Institute. They provided me with an idyllic environment for the completion of this book.

This work would not have been possible without the unstinting support of my family, particularly my parents Jeanette and Henry Glasser.

This book is dedicated to my wife Sharon and my children Noah and Abigail, who have enabled me to understand what is truly important.

1. Understanding the impact of exogenous revenues on political and economic reforms

Most Middle Easterners face puzzling political realities as they enter the new millennium. Robust Western-style democracies have not emerged in most of the Middle East, yet at the same time many countries throughout the region have experienced an important upsurge in political liberties during the last two decades. Throughout the 1990s Middle Eastern and Western intellectuals and scholars have debated the meaning of – and prospects for – democratic development in the Arab world, Iran and Turkey. These scholars have often overreacted to events in the region. In the late 1980s and early 1990s, some academics embraced a heady optimism regarding democratic developments in the region. It seemed then that the Middle East inevitably would benefit from the wave of democratization that was moving through much of Eastern Europe and the developing world. But by the end of the decade, many peoples of the region were facing renewed repression or a stalling of the political reform process. Consequently, by the end of the decade, the Middle East studies community came to embrace a decidedly pessimistic view on the prospects for democracy in the region. Analysts have begun to focus more on the Arab world's 'exceptionalism': its stubborn imperviousness to global trends toward increased democracy.

Often missing from their analyses has been an understanding of how and why political liberalization has evolved differently during particular times and in certain parts of the Middle East. Certainly, during the last 20 years, much of the region has experienced a political stasis or stagnation. Most Middle Eastern regimes have sought to extend highly circumscribed political rights to their populations. Yet predictably enough, these rulers have refused to allow this process to extend further – to evolve into *bona fide* democratization. But this liberalized-authoritarian stasis of the past two decades has assumed different manifestations in different parts of the region. At times, Middle Eastern authoritarians have enthusiastically embraced statist and expansionist economic policies and populist political coalitions. At other junctures, some regional regimes have oriented their statecraft around orthodox neoliberal economic policies and narrow right-wing political alliances. These differences have created powerfully divergent tendencies within the authoritarian stasis of the Middle East of the last 20 years. Yet our scholarly understanding of these trends remains extremely limited, obscured by a preoccupation with the question of whether global democratization processes have bypassed the region.

This book attempts to fill this intellectual gap by examining the ways in which Middle Eastern regimes have used controlled parliamentary politics to reinforce their economic development models. Here, this study contends, economic conditions and policies have often shaped political-liberalization processes in the region.

To wit, during the last 20 years several Middle Eastern countries have held elections in which opposition parties were permitted to compete freely for at least some of the seats. Not all of these elections had the same outcome. Some electoral designs favored center-right coalitions and some favored other groups. Consequently, center-right factions have controlled some parliaments whereas center-left, populist and sectarian groups have dominated other parliaments in the Middle East in the 1980s and 1990s.

Why have different Middle Eastern regimes favored different kinds of social groups in their electoral designs? Recent literature on democratic transitions suggests that internal political dynamics and elite politics in particular are crucial in determining the nature of electoral openings.[1] By contrast, this book shows that state access to external capital has had a critical impact on the design of electoral openings and on political liberalization and democratization in general. I focus on openings that occurred in Turkey, Morocco, Egypt, and Kuwait, but also consider important developments in other Middle Eastern countries.

I argue that Middle Eastern states lacking exogenous revenues (including oil revenues and foreign aid) have experienced severe fiscal crises and have created center-right and neoliberal parliamentary majorities. By contrast, I maintain, those states with greater exogenous resources have had milder economic crises and have developed more heterodox or populist electoral coalitions.

The nature of state revenues is critical in two respects. First, it has had a decisive impact on economic development. Middle Eastern states lacking exogenous revenues[2] have tended to be early and vigorous economic reformers. Those states commanding significant exogenous revenues (in other words, most Middle Eastern states) have tended to be late and weak reformers. Second, the structure of state revenue has shaped the development of parliamentary coalitions. Rent-poor states have had no choice but to ally with a center-right bourgeoisie that plays a pivotal role in the neoliberal economic reform program. Rent-rich regimes have avoided this strategy, preferring to maintain their alliances with more diverse social groups, especially the popular sectors. From these observations, I develop a typology of contemporary regional development based on the regime's adoption of development models and parliamentary coalitions. This framework extends the theories of the 'rentier state' literature, which contends that high levels of exogenous revenues have inhibited the liberalization and democratization of Middle Eastern polities.[3] But beyond the rentier state literature, my resource-based typology speaks to cross-regional debates on reformist economic and political trends in the developing world.

In the Middle East of the past 20 years, the driving force behind the adoption of neoliberal orthodoxy has been the foreign exchange crisis.[4] States experiencing such crises have been inclined to implement economic reforms to maintain solvency and avert economic collapse. States with access to exogenous revenues – particularly those that do not flow from the international financial institutions – have been better able to avoid foreign exchange crises and therefore have been less inclined to implement neoliberal reforms.

Exogenous windfalls, so long as they come from 'nonconditional' sources, typically prompt states to increase statist and populist expenditures.[5] Conversely, precipitous drops in foreign exchange earnings tend to prompt states – even some rent-rich ones like Algeria – to initiate economic reform. But in general, states commanding considerable exogenous revenues or nonconditional finance (as a percentage of total state revenues) will tend to backslide on their reforms and resume their populist programs once macroeconomic balance has been restored. By contrast, states losing most of their exogenous resources (typically because of the discontinuation of foreign aid) are more apt to become consistent and serious economic reformers.[6]

My conceptualizations of Middle Eastern development do reflect the link between economic reforms and the nature of the state. I am, above all, examining prospects for economic reform in polities controlled by relatively strong and stable state structures. Most Middle Eastern countries have had such structures, ones that are able to formulate and implement development policies. (Exceptions to the regional norm of stable state structures have included war-torn and fragmented polities such as Sudan, Lebanon, and post-unification Yemen.) Consequently, my framework explains a regional development pattern, since the effects of exogenous resources are clearly visible across the major Middle Eastern states, which tend to be stable and cohesive.

In turn, this study explains electoral outcomes in liberalizing Middle Eastern polities; in other words, those states permitting significant independent political activity and competitive elections for at least some parliamentary seats. One of my central assumptions is that liberalizing regimes design openings that privilege socioeconomic groups or class actors whose cooperation is critical to the regime's development programs.[7] Liberalizing regimes facing critical gaps in foreign exchange have no choice but to ensure that the electoral process favors leading business and merchant groups with links to international capital. In countries with relatively abundant exogenous resources, liberalizing regimes have tended to develop parliamentary coalitions that favor populist groups or nonclass actors.

SHOULD THE MIDDLE EAST BE INCORPORATED INTO GLOBAL STUDIES OF DEMOCRATIC TRANSITIONS?

The current global wave of democratization, which began in 1974, has generated perhaps the most substantive research program in comparative politics. One of the more intriguing aspects of this enterprise is its cross-regional scope. In contributing to a lively debate, scholars have compared the surge in democratic regimes in regions as diverse as Latin America, Eastern and Southern Asia, and Southern and Eastern Europe. Though emphasizing the distinctiveness of trends within particular regions and countries, they have succeeded to a great extent in incorporating a common set of terms and concepts, and in underscoring important interregional developments. When confronted by the absence of Middle Eastern cases from most of these analyses, it is possible to give a straightforward explanation: the emerging literature on democratic transitions has ignored the Middle East, simply because the global democratization trend has on the whole bypassed the region. But of course the region's 'exceptionalism,'[8] as one analyst put it, is far from complete. Though perhaps suggesting their own development typology, Middle Eastern cases do have a basis for a comparison with political openings in other world regions, not in terms of democratization *per se*, but in terms of political liberalization. That process, which exists in states containing most of the Middle Eastern population,[9] has become a defining element of the region's political development. In constituting 'an usual departure from the usual practice of authoritarian regimes,' as Guillermo O'Donnell and Philipe Schmitter put it,[10] liberalization is a key component of any political opening.

Middle Eastern regimes, like those in other world regions, open their polities in response to some kind of crisis. Political openings, in the Middle East or elsewhere, tend not to occur during times of economic prosperity and political equanimity. As O'Donnell and Schmitter observe, if things are going well, and no important crises or challenges are foreseen, why decide on changes that will inevitably introduce new actors and uncertainties, however tightly liberalization may be controlled by the regime? Typically, regime elites calculate that a political opening, or some form of 'electoral legitimation,'[11] is needed to stabilize their control over the political system. They calculate that an opening will be more effective in assuaging popular demands upon the regime than will increased repression or the perpetuation of the status quo.

Thus, as I argue in this study, regional examples speak to the cross-regional issues of transition modalities and the sequencing of political and economic reform. In short, one might fruitfully compare the regional 'species' of political liberalization with the global 'genus' of democratic transitions, all the while remembering Giovani Sartori's admonition that scholars must make appropriate conceptual adjustments in their cross-regional comparisons.[12] Indeed, such a comparison is particularly apt, in that most Middle Eastern political openings, like most of those throughout the Third World, are shaped by the pressures of economic crisis and reform.

THE IMPACT OF EXOGENOUS REVENUES ON ELECTORAL OPENINGS: BUILDING ON THE DEMOCRATIC TRANSITIONS LITERATURE

My understanding of political reform contrasts sharply with recent themes in the democratic transitions literature, which emphasizes the importance of elite politics and regime-opposition relations in electoral openings. Guillermo O'Donnell, Philippe Schmitter and Laurence Whitehead's *Transitions from Authoritarian Rule*, the landmark collection of studies of redemocratization in Latin America and Southern Europe, firmly established the centrality of 'domestic, internal factors'[13] in debates about the nature of political openings. These volumes, published in 1986, focused on divisions within authoritarian regimes, the interests and fears of incumbents and opposition leaders, the mobilization of civil society, and the relevance of pacts in consolidating democratic rule.[14] A few contributions emphasizing political economy were the exceptions within *Transitions from Authoritarian Rule*. For example, Terry Karl argued that oil wealth helped to consolidate the Venezuelan democratic transition that occurred in 1958, by enabling the state to alleviate destabilizing social demands.[15] But on the whole, the O'Donnell, Schmitter and Whitehead volumes consciously de-emphasized 'macro structural factors' and established the primacy of political elites in the analysis of democratic transitions.[16] Their emphasis on strategic interactions was an effort to break with the scholarship of the 1960s and 1970s, which argued that economic structures and preconditions determined democratic development.[17]

Consequently, a dominant theme in the current literature is the analysis of different 'modes of transition.' In the 1990s, drawing on the *Transitions* volumes, scholars have argued that political openings tend to result from divisions between hard- and soft-liners within the ruling elite, and that the subsequent transitions are shaped by negotiations among the elite factions and the leading opposition groups.[18] For example, Adam Przewoski translated the O'Donnell–Schmitter model into game-theoretic language in his comparison of transitions in Eastern Europe and Latin America. He outlined a series of strategic calculations made by four critical actors in a democratic transition: the hard-liners and the soft-liners in the regime, and the moderates and the radicals in the opposition.[19]

Similarly, Scott Mainwaring, Guillermo O'Donnell and J. Samuel Valenzuela developed a tripartite typology of the degree to which the old regime is able to control the opposition and the transition. In cases like Spain and Brazil, where the outgoing rulers retain a high degree of power, a 'transition through transaction' occurs without many of the rules of the regime being broken. At the other extreme, in cases such as Portugal, Greece, and Argentina, the collapse of the old regime leads to a 'transaction through defeat.' Here the outgoing leaders are completely unable to control the opening or negotiate their withdrawal from power. The intermediate category is a 'transition through extrication' in which the rules of the authoritarian regime are abolished, but the rulers are able to negotiate their abdication.[20] Using different terminology, Samuel Huntington developed a similar typology of the modes of transition.[21] In turn, debate has revolved around the question of whether different modes of transition indeed lead to different kinds of institutions in the emergent regimes.[22]

In short, current debates about democratization have focused almost exclusively on the process of strategic choices, and have ignored the broader contexts embracing that process. In this sense, critics have observed, the transitions literature has become overly voluntaristic.[23] Naturally enough, this literature has overlooked the effects of radically different economic conditions, not to mention the nature and structure of state revenue, on regimes' designs of political openings.

THE RENTIER STATE: TOWARD A MIDDLE EASTERN PARADIGM?

This section examines the insights of the rentier state literature, which has underscored the importance of exogenous revenues in Middle Eastern political development. The reformulation of rentier state conceptualizations, I argue below, allows one to understand how external capital affects political openings.

Most Middle Eastern countries are unusually dependent on external capital that accrues directly to the state. Instead of taxing their populations, Middle Eastern governments rely on such external sources as oil revenues, grants, loans, and pipeline and canal fees. As the dominant framework for the interpretation of the contemporary regional political economy, the rentier state literature argues that the lack of dependence on taxation precludes the rise of popular demands for political participation. For example, Hossein Mahdavy, Jacques Delacroix, Jill Crystal, Lisa Anderson, Hazem Beblawi, and Giacomo Luciani argue that regimes with access to exogenous rents are insulated from domestic (and to a lesser extent, international) pressures for political reform and democratization.[24] These scholars argue that in the Middle East there is 'no representation without taxation.'[25] Beblawi and Luciani argue that a state is more or less rentier, on the basis of its receiving relatively high or low levels of external or nonproductive revenues.[26] In short, they maintain, the greater the availability of rents, the lesser the demands for political liberalization and democratization.[27]

Here their conceptual logic is simple. Because of their external income sources, these 'rentier states' need not extract significant revenues from their populations. (Middle Eastern taxation rates on income, profits, and capital gains are among the lowest in the world, as IMF and World Bank studies repeatedly have demonstrated.[28]) The availability of exogenous rents enables the state to become the central, and in some cases, highly generous, distributor of goods and services. In turn, the state elite uses patronage, or the provision of welfare, to buy the population's loyalty or political quiescence.

The organization of the rentier society is, as Luciani puts it, not characterized by production and extraction, but by allocation and consumption. Consequently, popular demands for governmental accountability, and for participation in the political system, tend not to develop. Reliance on state largesse prevents the population from developing a democratic mindset, or at any rate from demanding political representation.[29]

The literature also argues that the rentier state has peculiar bureaucratic and developmental features. The institutions of the Middle Eastern state tend to be oriented around the distribution of patronage instead of the extraction of resources from society.[30] Likewise, Michael Chatelus contends, the rentier state promotes consumption and socioeconomic stability over progressive policies generating economic development, industrialization, and 'modern' class relations.[31] In the end, the rulers' command over exogenous resources has altered and, in some sense, distorted both 'normal' economic development and mechanisms for political representation in Middle Eastern states.

The archetypal rentier states are the Persian/Arabian Gulf oil monarchies, whose governments use vast oil-generated revenues to control comparatively tiny populations. But as Beblawi and Luciani observe, the region's larger and poorer countries also have rentier qualities, as their governments receive substantial proportions of their revenues from external sources. They attribute the spread of the 'rentier effect' to a regional 'system' that redistributes oil-generated wealth among the Arab states. By and large, such a redistribution has assumed the form of inter-Arab foreign aid and expatriate workers' remittances. But other sources typically include locational rents such as pipeline and canal fees; revenue from 'non-productive' domestic industries engaged in different kinds of mineral extraction; and aid from Western donors and creditors. Consequently, as Beblawi and Luciani argue, the rentier state is a regional paradigm, one speaking to political development in almost all Middle Eastern states.[32]

DEVELOPING THE RENTIER STATE LITERATURE

In focusing on a factor militating against political liberalization and democratization, the 'rentier state' literature does not properly address how the states of the region experience these processes, if and when they do. As it turns out, the rulers' access to exogenous revenues does not in itself prevent reform and democratization from occurring. Much of the early literature, in neglecting this fact, has a static quality, as Middle Eastern states are presumed to be perpetually locked into authoritarian cycles.[33]

Recently, analysts have noted that economic decline or economic crisis may compel regimes, particularly those receiving more modest proportions of their revenues from exogenous sources, to open up their political systems. Patrick Clawson, Daniel Brumberg, and Mustapha Said, for example, argue that Middle Eastern regimes facing economic crises have extended political liberties to appease citizenries angered by the rollback of populist economic rights.[34] Consequently, as Clawson and Alan Richards and John Waterbury note, the adoption of neoliberal economic policies has coincided with political liberalizations in countries throughout the region.[35] But beyond such observations, the existing literature does not offer a precise and rigorous interpretation of the impact of state revenue sources and economic change on regional processes of political liberalization, democratization, and redemocratization.[36]

Regimes in Morocco, Turkey, Tunisia, Egypt, and Kuwait all staged landmark political openings in the 1980s. But why did rent-poor Morocco, Turkey, and Tunisia favor electoral coalitions espousing neoliberal economic policies, whereas rent-dependent Egypt developed a more populist parliamentary constellation, and oil-rich Kuwait installed groups calling for even more expansionary and heterodox economic programs? Each regime, through political liberalization, apparently sought to legitimate a distinctive development model.[37] Scholars such as Beblawi and Luciani acknowledge that oil-rich and oil-poor states create dramatically different patterns of political participation.[38] Yet the existing regional literature on political development, which purports to explain how and why Middle Eastern regimes liberalize, does not offer a formalized or systematic explanation of these differences across countries with radically different state revenue structures. That is, leading theorists of the paradigm do not explain how rulers with access to extremely high levels of exogenous revenues (say, 95 percent of total government revenue) structure political openings that are different from those developed by rulers with access to more modest levels of exogenous revenues (say, 35 percent of total government revenues). In a word, applications of the rentier-state hypothesis lack comparative rigor.

HYPOTHESES AND ASSUMPTIONS

I argue that a pattern is discernible in the impact of exogenous revenues on political development in countries throughout the Middle East. That impact has radically different, even polar opposite, ramifications in different types of political economies in the region.

My framework contends that the structure of state revenue prompts state elites to favor one development policy over another, and therefore to favor one socioeconomic group over another in the political system. Here the nature of state revenue sources is important, because it shapes the regime's ability to cope with economic change and crisis. In a word, it decisively influences the rulers' attempt to advantage and disadvantage particular socioeconomic groups in the opening of the political system.

I hypothesize that the lower the level of the regime's exogenous rents, the more inclined the regime will be to favor center-right bourgeois groups in the electoral process and in the political system in general.

My hypothesis presumes that the more the regime is forced to incorporate a center-right bourgeoisie, or important business or merchant groups, within a neoliberal development strategy, the more the regime will provide such strata with a meaningful electoral-political role.

It also presumes that the lower the level of the regime's exogenous revenues, the more likely the regime will be to implement a neoliberal development model.

Though building on the existing literature, my approach is unique, in that it attempts to develop a systematic understanding of the link between electoral politics and state revenue sources in different countries throughout the region. Like O'Donnell and Schmitter, I recognize that a range of different factors and crises may compel regimes to liberalize their polities.[39] But unlike most of the literature, which focuses on *whether* Middle Eastern regimes liberalize and democratize, I am concerned primarily with *how* they do so. My main interest is, in short, the dynamics of political reform and the mechanisms through which certain groups are favored in that process. Here, flows of state revenue are critical, for rent-impoverished regimes have no choice but to give the dominant parliamentary role to a neoliberal coalition. By contrast, regimes receiving high levels of exogenous revenues tend to develop alternative parliamentary alliances, especially those favoring populist groups and nonclass actors.

I presume that regimes balance dual pressures of legitimation and accumulation. All four regimes faced crises in the early 1980s, and I am describing their attempts to legitimate different development policies. That legitimation effort, I argue, was best expressed in the political opening that occurred in each country's parliament, a venue in which the regime seeks to define modes of popular political participation.

THE CENTER-RIGHT

'Center-right' refers to those bourgeois groups that advocate, or stand to benefit from, an orthodox economic development program. In my use of the concept, center-right economic policies typically militate against the immediate interests of the working classes and popular sectors, and promote those of business or merchant groups, especially those seeking to benefit from ties to international capital. Such policies, moreover, are part and parcel of the economic neoliberalism promoted globally by the World Bank and the International Monetary Fund.[40]

In particular, center-right economic programs tend to include: the lowering of inflation and budget deficits; the easing of balance-of-payments problems; the reduction (or elimination) of government consumer subsidies; the reduction of government spending in general; the privatization of state enterprises and the promotion of the private sector; the rollback of welfarism and government intervention in the economy; trade liberalization and integration into the global economy; and a range of policies designed to promote export-led growth and to dismantle established import-substituting development models.[41]

In general, such policies are double-edged. They prescribe austerity for the popular sectors (at least for the short term), and confer rewards and incentives upon select private-sector groups.[42] Of course, to an extent, my conceptualization of orthodoxy or neoliberalism is idealized. Across Middle Eastern polities, specific center-right programs tend to share the above characteristics. Yet they also may deviate somewhat on specific issues from the basic prescriptions of neoliberalism. Still, on my definition, crucial elements of a right-wing program include its favoring of an upper bourgeoisie, and its evisceration of the power of the popular, working, or 'disadvantaged' sectors.

Middle Eastern electoral experiments of the 1980s and the 1990s are targeted increasingly at a center-right bourgeoisie because of two overriding factors. First, the decline of import-substitution industrialization (ISI) throughout the Third World, and the concomitant rise of an orthodox macroeconomic consensus among the international creditor community have shaped political openings throughout the developing world.[43]

For example, the Moroccan and Turkish governments, like others throughout the Third World, have received powerful international incentives during the 1980s to create political systems that legitimate efficient and export-oriented economic activity, and that hinder the political effectiveness of popular-sector groups.

Second, in the case of the Arab states, the oil glut of the 1980s has decreased the level of exogenous rents available to the regimes, both by decreasing the profitability of petroleum industries and by staunching foreign aid flows within the region.

Thus, my research presumes that the oil glut and the crisis in Third World ISI models have pushed most rent-poor regimes in the region to recast the tenor of political life. Put baldly, in the 1950s, 1960s and 1970s, Middle Eastern regimes attempted to destroy bourgeois groups – or at least, to lock them out of political life. As well, in this period all Middle Eastern states pursued intense statist development policies. By contrast, because of the economic austerity and the crisis in ISI development models of the 1980s and 1990s, the regimes now have targeted leading bourgeois groups for a relatively privileged political position. Here the logic is relatively simple. International donors and creditors have compelled Middle Eastern states to adopt increasingly neoliberal development models. In turn, regimes attempt to coopt or accommodate center-right bourgeois groups through a controlled electoral opening, since these groups have resources that the regimes need for their development programs. In other words, as exogenous rent flows have declined and as ISI models have faltered, such groups have become relatively more important to regimes pursuing increasingly orthodox development strategies.

In brief, my hypothesis recasts the core conceptualizations of the 'rentier state' literature. Most of the existing literature focuses on the notion that state access to exogenous rents militates against political liberalization and democratization *per se*. My hypothesis, by contrast, is that such access militates against the adoption of neoliberalism and the favoring of an electoral coalition representing a center-right bourgeoisie. Rulers of states receiving significant exogenous resources (for example, Kuwait and Egypt of the 1980s) create political openings that favor populist coalitions and nonclass actors, because they believe such openings will stabilize and legitimate their regimes. Typically, in facing crises, such regimes need to broaden and popularize their alliances, and they attempt to do so with populist development models and political openings. By contrast, rent-impoverished regimes do not have this ability.

My research examines the link between reformist economic and political pressures within countries that represent three predominant kinds of political-economic configurations. It considers Kuwait as an example of electoral politics in a 'highly rentier' system, Egypt as an example of electoral politics in a 'semi-rentier' system, and Turkey and Morocco as examples of electoral politics in 'minimally rentier' systems. My primary concern is how an authoritarian regime seeks to liberalize or democratize. Accordingly, I focus largely, though not exclusively, on four particular political openings: the Kuwaiti reinstatement of electoral politics in 1981; the resumption of the Egyptian electoral process in 1984 (following the severe setbacks to political liberalization during 1979–81); Turkish redemocratization during 1982–3, and the landmark Moroccan parliamentary elections in 1984.

I have selected these four cases, because they are exemplars of their categories: in each case the roles of bourgeois and center-right groups in the electoral experiments are clearly cast. Furthermore, in facing crises and in staging political openings in the early 1980s, each regime developed policies that continued to shape political and economic development throughout the decade and into the 1990s. As I show in my conclusion, subsequent elections in these countries and in other liberalizing Middle Eastern states are compatible with my hypotheses, even though they may not correspond to the parameters of my framework as clearly as the four cases that I have chosen.

A POLITICAL-ECONOMIC FRAMEWORK FOR THE INTERPRETATION OF MIDDLE EASTERN ELECTORAL EXPERIMENTS DURING THE 1980s AND 1990s

1. *The 'minimally rentier' states:* for example, Turkey and Morocco. Exogenous revenues comprised less than 20 percent of Moroccan and Turkish state revenues in the two years preceding the political openings in these countries.[44] (Foreign aid provided these two states with most of their exogenous resources; however, a Moroccan phosphate industry and a Turkish oil pipeline did generate additional exogenous revenues for the governments.) These countries faced serious economic crises and resource gaps during the late 1970s and early 1980s, and were forced to embrace the neoliberal policies of international donors and creditors. In turn, each regime designed an electoral system that blatantly favored center-right bourgeois groups, thus enabling them to dominate the parliament.

Of major Middle Eastern states, Turkey and Morocco have been among the most rent-impoverished. Consequently, they have implemented economic reform, and favored the center-right, to the greatest extent during the 1980s.

1(a) *The (relatively) democratic alternative:* Turkey. During the redemocratization process of 1982–4, the junta helps to engineer the parliamentary dominance of orthodox-oriented center-right bourgeois groups. That is, such groups are given an ascendant position within the new democratic regime.

1(b) *The pluralistic-authoritarian alternative:* Morocco. In buttressing its policy of macroeconomic liberalism, the monarchy ensures in 1984 that pro-orthodox parties and groups dominate the parliament, and at the same time preserves extensive authoritarian control over society.

2. *The 'semi-rentier' state:* for example, Egypt. Exogenous revenues equaled roughly 45 percent of total Egyptian revenues during the early 1980s.[45] During this period, exogenous revenues enabled an insecure regime to indulge popular sector interests and to postpone economic reforms. In the defining 1984 parliamentary elections, the posturing of the regime's National Democratic Party (NDP) strongly reflected the government's interest in mollifying popular-sector demands.

Unlike the minimally rentier states, semi-rentier Egypt was able to use exogenous rents to forestall both far-reaching macroeconomic orthodoxy and the blatant favoring of bourgeois groups in the electoral-political system. In sum, the regime preserved its 'center-left' parliamentary predominance *and* used center-right bourgeois opposition in parliament to portray itself as a protector of the popular sectors.

At the same time, however, the Egyptian economy faced the dangers of long-term economic stagnation and decline. Consequently, the support and resources of center-right bourgeois groups were, and remain, critical to the development strategy of the semi-rentier Egyptian state. It therefore sought to give these groups a privileged though *oppositional* role within the parliament, and attempted to coopt them within both the parliamentary and economic reform processes.

3. *The 'highly rentier' state:* for example, Kuwait. Such a state receives at least 75 percent, and often over 90 percent of their revenues from exogenous sources.[46] Here the parliamentary process is typically used to dilute and undermine the political power of bourgeois groups, which may make threatening political demands against the regime, and whose resources are unimportant to the regime's development program. Furthermore, the highly rentier state uses exogenous revenues to build extensive alliances to legitimate the regime in the eyes of the citizenry. These dynamics were keenly displayed in the Kuwaiti parliament of the 1980s. The Kuwaiti regime has been able to use an optimal legitimation strategy, in the sense that poorer governments tend to replicate it, albeit to a lesser extent, whenever they happen to have the (exogenous) resources. Further, unlike the other states, the highly rentier one

is able to marginalize bourgeois groups in the parliament, since it does not need their participation in the government development strategy.

INTERPRETING THE PARLIAMENTARY PROCESS

The electoral and legislative processes have somewhat different functions in each of the four cases. The greatest difference is between the democratic Turkish case and the authoritarian Moroccan, Egyptian, and Kuwaiti ones. That is, in the Turkish case, the parliament's chief function has been the making of state policy. In the other cases, generally speaking, the parliaments have had lesser powers. Is there a common basis, then, for comparing electoral-political processes in all four cases?

My main concern is the ability of social groups to voice their opinions, press their demands, and thereby secure a measure of participation in the electoral-political system. Here I am not only interested in policy-making and power-sharing *per se*, but also in the ability of social groups to maximize the opportunities of electoral processes and political liberalization. I assume that electoral experiments in the four cases matter, to the extent that they establish distinctive patterns of political participation.

In short, a regime affords better opportunities for political expression and participation to those social groups whose support is central to the regime's development program. Here the exercise of limited political and civil liberties is the critical commonality in the elections considered in each of the four cases. Political liberalization provides significant but limited opportunities for oppositional activities in the context of independent political associations. At most, such liberalization provides the opposition with (limited) opportunities to share power and shape policy-making. More typically, political participation in a liberalizing polity includes opportunities for opposition groups to have a significant parliamentary representation, to have limited checks on the arbitrary exercise of power, and to exercise limited freedoms of expression and dissent. Both scholars and civil rights organizations recognize that 'liberalized authoritarianism'[47] is a distinctive and measurable category that includes neither entirely repressive nor essentially democratic regimes.

Of course, I do not in any way seek to obscure the important difference between Turkish redemocratization and Arab liberalization in the 1980s. I am particularly sensitive to the fact that competitive elections determined the fate of Turkish rulers, whereas such a genuine competition for power did not exist in the Arab cases. Nevertheless, a critical commonality exists in terms of how the authoritarian Turkish and Arab regimes of the early 1980s structured opportunities for political expression and participation. In both cases, the regimes carefully used electoral controls to determine the status of groups in the political system.

In 1983, the Turkish military regime did permit the return of democracy, yet its control of that process was tight, precise, and highly exclusionary, especially in its bias against the left. Thus, in comparing the Arab and Turkish political openings, I am comparing the regimes' authoritarian design of the electoral process.

All the regimes, in brief, implemented strategies of empowerment and exclusion with a fair degree of success. Each authoritarian regime sought to weaken or strengthen existing parties or factions through a redesign of the electoral system, to help or hinder particular parties or factions by using government resources disproportionately, to block certain groups from participation altogether, and sometimes to sponsor or create new (dominant) parties. In this context, the Turkish, Moroccan, Egyptian, and Kuwaiti elections all offered their voting publics highly circumscribed and manipulated choices among parties, candidates, and policy preferences.

In the Moroccan and Turkish cases, economic crisis and low levels of exogenous rents ultimately meant that bourgeois groups in parliament were able to make strident appeals for macroeconomic orthodoxy. These groups exploited these opportunities by appealing for 'capitalist' and 'technocratic' policies – for example, privatization – that served their interests. Since their interests coincided with the perceived 'accumulation' requirements of the regime, these groups were given an ascendant position in the electoral-political system.

In the event, by benefiting from the Turkish junta's anti-populist legal and electoral codes, the Motherland Party was able to champion the continuation of austerity measures implemented by the military regime in 1980. Likewise, the Constitutional Union (UC) used its parliamentary dominance to promote the austerity package that the Moroccan government negotiated with its international creditors in 1983. Furthermore, the crown's provision of support, patronage, and legitimacy was in itself instrumental in the electoral triumph of the UC, a party devoted to the interests of the urban bourgeoisie. That is, center-right bourgeois groups were best able to exercise the 'rights' of political expression that were proffered by the electoral openings of the region's minimally rentier states.

Unlike the Turkish and Moroccan regimes, the Egyptian regime provided in 1984 not for the electoral success of a center-right party (in this case, the New Wafd), but for the parliamentary victory of the (state's) center-left National Democratic Party. The New Wafd gained neither special access to the regime nor a dominant electoral-political position from which it could champion its preferred macroeconomic policies. Instead, the New Wafd was the only opposition group permitted to win parliamentary representation. Egypt qua semi-rentier state did not offer a pro-orthodox bourgeoisie a chance to join in, let alone form, a government; for much of the regime's leadership in fact opposes far-reaching economic liberalization. Rather, the New Wafd was forced to be a 'corrective' and 'complementary'[48] opposition that enabled the regime to portray itself as a protector of the popular sector. In the end, the regime ensured that the dominant electoral-political voice was the 'center-left' one of the National Democratic Party (NDP).

By contrast, the Kuwaiti electoral opening of 1981 exemplified the political liberalization process in a highly rentier polity: the regime had the luxury of giving bourgeois groups a decidedly peripheral role in the design and implementation of the electoral experiment. In the event, the regime used electoral manipulations to empower tribal Beduin allies who tended to be hostile toward Kuwait's urban bourgeoisie. More generally, over the decades the Kuwaiti regime has used the parliamentary process to effect the political decline of the urban economic elite, and to provide Beduin tribal allies with patronage in exchange for their electoral support. Here ethnic and socioeconomic identities have overlapped, as Beduins have been the least privileged sector of the Kuwaiti citizenry, while urban Sunni merchant families have comprised the Kuwaiti economic elite. The electoral design of the 1980s served to augment and consolidate the long-term political decline of this upper bourgeoisie.

THE SCOPE AND LIMITATIONS OF THE FRAMEWORK

My framework presumes that distinctive electoral forms are likely to emerge in countries representing different regional political-economic configurations. My tripartite typology reflects the peculiar nature of regional economic austerity during the 1980s and 1990s, and in this sense is time-bound. My theorizing is not necessarily relevant to the previous development period, in which all regimes pursued populist and interventionist economic policies.

As well, my framework generalizes about a political-economic process that exists throughout the Middle East, from Morocco to the Gulf. This developmental process cuts across regime types: in other words, monarchy, authoritarian republic, and democracy. The cases of Turkey and Morocco offer perhaps the most striking example of this dynamic, as I argue above.

Further, in elaborating on how exogenous rents shape regional development trends, I attempt to explain how a particular set of issues is uniquely relevant to Middle Eastern politics. Of course, in other world areas, state reliance on exogenous rents is an important feature of political development.[49] At the same time, such revenues have had a uniquely important impact on political development in the Middle East, largely because almost all the countries in the region have received unusually large amounts of such revenues.

Scholars have yet to develop sophisticated interregional comparisons of exogenous resources, but some dramatic indices do exist. A few scholars working with the paradigm have noted that Middle Eastern direct taxes on incomes, profits, and capital gains are among the lowest in the world. James Bill and Robert Springborg note that

> while in 1988 in the US, Japan, and Canada, such taxes amounted to 50 percent, 68.8 percent, and 48.5 percent of total current revenues, respectively, in Egypt these taxes accounted for 15.2 percent, in Tunisia for 12.2 percent, and in Yemen for 13.3 percent of revenues.[50]

According to the World Bank, Third World countries as a whole received roughly one-quarter of their revenues from direct taxes. Yet in the Middle East, only Turkey and Israel acquired more than 20 percent of their revenues from such taxes. Among Arab countries, only Morocco and Egypt obtained over 15 percent of their revenues from direct taxes during the mid-1980s.[51]

Additional interesting, though potentially misleading, World Bank data concern nontax revenues. This statistic includes some internal sources of revenue, for example, from state-owned enterprises; and excludes some exogenous rents, such as foreign aid. Nevertheless, the data make for an interesting comparison, since almost all Middle Eastern countries receive dramatically inflated levels of nontax revenues from state-owned extractive exogenous industries. That is, almost all Middle Eastern states typically receive more than 20 percent of their revenues from non-tax sources,[52] the exceptions being the minimally rentier cases of Turkey and Morocco. World Bank studies of the 1980s and 1990s have shown that about one-quarter of the world's states, including those of the Middle East, receive more than 20 percent of their income from nontax sources. Furthermore, roughly half of the world's states in this category are Middle Eastern; the rest are from various world regions. Such states, in sum, represent the norm in the Middle East, but are unusual from a comparative global perspective. Finally, from such a global perspective, even the region's minimally rentier states rely on relatively high levels of nontax revenues.[53]

Exogenous rents have worked, in conjunction with other factors, to create distinct development patterns in the Middle East. They have, in other regions, similarly worked to enhance state strength and autonomy. But substantial levels of exogenous rents have, in cases from other regions, coincided with different developmental sequences; hence, they have had different ramifications for political development.

For example, Terry Karl argues that oil revenues have enabled the

Venezuelan state to provide largesse to key constituents, and, since 1958, have helped to consolidate a pacted democracy in that country. Venezuela, consequently, has been an unusual example of democratic stability in Latin America.[54] Conversely, in Middle Eastern cases, exogenous rents have typically enhanced various kinds of authoritarian regimes. One implication is that unusually high levels of exogenous rents tend to stabilize an existing regime, be it democratic or authoritarian. (They tend to do so because they work to insulate the regime from destabilizing economic shocks and enable it to buy the political quiescence of the population.) In non-Middle Eastern cases, because of different developmental factors, unusually high levels of exogenous rents have been used to promote activities that support different kinds of regimes (for example, pacted democratic ones).

The analysis of the impact of exogenous rents, in sum, is one systematic approach among many such approaches to the comparative study of Middle Eastern political systems. I am contending that a formalized understanding of the relationship between exogenous rents and political development will better enable regionalists to explore why and how the political development of the region is, and has been, distinct.

Indeed, much regional scholarship has tended to emphasize the cultural distinctiveness of the Middle East. Comparativists such as Samuel Huntington have called for the creation of regional development models, on the basis of cultural groupings.[55] In the Middle East, he and other scholars contend, that model should emphasize Arab and Islamic culture.

My point is that generalizations, cultural or otherwise, about contemporary Middle Eastern politics cannot be divorced entirely from the issue of exogenous revenues, which have a pervasive effect on the development of the region's regimes. An understanding of exogenous revenues enables one to explain how political development in most Middle Eastern states has differed from political development in other world regions.

In the end, levels of exogenous revenue work to create the political-economic structures in which Middle Eastern regimes make decisions about the nature of political participation. That is, they make the emergence of certain forms of political openings highly probable. Regional electoral experiments, as engineered by regime elites, demonstrate a rough pattern of structured contingent choice. Consequently, to borrow the phrase of a student of Latin America, I am suggesting 'a contextually bounded approach'[56] to the study of Middle Eastern political change.

In a word, levels of exogenous revenues have created a distinctive regional paradigm, one reflecting the poles of neoliberalism and statism. Yet the effects of these resources are not specifically Middle Eastern. This study seeks to show how exogenous revenues may well shape the political and economic reforms of countries throughout the developing world.

NOTES

1. Here the seminal statement is Guillermo O'Donnell and Philippe Schmitter, *Transitions from Authoritarian Rule: Tentative Conclusions about Uncertain Democracies*, Baltimore, MD: Johns Hopkins University Press, 1986.
2. 'Exogenous revenue' is generally defined as state income from external and 'non-productive' sources, including foreign aid, expatriate labor remittances, overseas investments, bank loans, and the extraction of non-renewable assets, particularly oil. Hazem Beblawi and Giacomo Luciani (eds), *Nation, State and Integration in the Arab World: The Rentier State*, London: Croom Helm, 1987, p. 51.
3. Ibid.
4. See, for example, Henri J. Barkey, 'State Autonomy and the Crisis of Import Substitution,' *Comparative Political Studies*, 2(3) (October 1989) 291–314; Stephan Haggard and Robert Kaufman, 'The Politics of Stabilization and Structural Adjustment,' in Jeffrey Sachs (ed.), *Developing Country Debt and Economic Performance: The International Financial System*, Chicago: University of Chicago Press, 1989.
5. John Waterbury, 'The Political Management of Economic Adjustment and Reform,' in his *Politics of Public Sector Reform and Privatization*, Boulder, CO: Westview Press, 1990, p. 49; and Miles Kahler, 'External Influence, Conditionality, and the Politics of Adjustment,' in Haggard and Kaufman, *The Politics of Economic Adjustment*, p. 111.
6. Chapter 2 explicates this dynamic. Or see my 'External Capital and Political Liberalizations,' *Journal of International Affairs*, 49 (Summer 1995), 45–74.
7. Robert Kaufman observed this about political openings in Latin America in 'Liberalization and Democratization in South America: Perspectives from the 1970s,' in O'Donnell and Schmitter, *Transitions from Authoritarian Rule*, Baltimore, MD: Johns Hopkins University Press, 1986.
8. Mustapha Said, 'The New Face of Authoritarianism in the Arab World,' unpublished paper, 1.
9. Michael Hudson, 'After the Gulf War: Prospects for Democratization in the Arab World,' *Middle East Journal*, 49(3), Summer 1991, 407–26.
10. O'Donnell and Schmitter, *Transitions from Authoritarian Rule*, p. 7.
11. Ibid., p. 17.
12. Sartori, as cited in Gerardo Munck, in 'Issues in Democratic Consolidation: the New South American Democracies in Comparative Perspective,' *Comparative Politics*, 26(3) (April 1994), 374.
13. O'Donnell and Schmitter, *Transitions from Authoritarian Rule*, p. 18.
14. Guillermo O'Donnell, Philippe Schmitter, and Laurence Whitehead (eds), *Transitions from Authoritarian Rule: Comparative Perspectives*; *Transitions from Authoritarian Rule: Southern Europe*; *Transitions from Authoritarian Rule: Latin America*, 3 vols, Baltimore, MD: Johns Hopkins University Press, 1986.
15. Terry Lynn Karl, 'Petroleum and Political Pacts: the Transition to Democracy in Venezuela,' in O'Donnell *et al.*, Vol. 2, pp. 196–220.
16. O'Donnell and Schmitter, *Transitions from Authoritarian Rule*, p. 19.
17. Much of the transitions literature was written in response to the structural bureaucratic-authoritarian model of Guillermo O'Donnell in his *Modernization and Bureaucratic Authoritarianism*, Berkeley, CA: Institute of International Studies, University of California, 1979.
18. See, for example, Scott Mainwaring, Guillermo O'Donnell, and J. Samuel Valenzuela (eds), *Issues in Democratic Consolidation: The New South American Democracies in Comparative Perspective*, South Bend, IN: University of Notre Dame Press, 1992.
19. Adam Przeworski, *Democracy and the Market: Political and Economic Reforms in Eastern Europe and Latin America*, Cambridge: Cambridge University Press, 1991.
20. As summarized by Munck, 'Democratic Transitions,' 358.
21. Samuel Huntington, *The Third Wave: Democratization in the Late Twentieth Century*, Norman, OK: University of Oklahoma Press, 1991, pp. 114–15.

22. See Munck's discussion, 'Democratic Transitions,' 358–65.
23. See, for example, Terry Lynn Karl, 'Dilemmas of Democratization in Latin America,' *Comparative Politics*, 23(1) (1990), 1–21.
24. Early discussions of this notion are in Hossein Mahdavy, 'The Patterns and Problems of Economic Development in Rentier States: the Case of Iran,' in M.A. Cook (ed.), *Studies in the Economic History in the Middle East*, New York: Oxford University Press, 1970; and in Jacques Delacroix, 'The Distributive State in the World System,' *Studies in Comparative International Development*, 15 (1980), 3–21. Later formulations are found in Lisa Anderson, 'The State in the Middle East and North Africa,' *Comparative Politics*, 20(1) (October 1987), 9–10; in Hazem Beblawi and Giacomo Luciani (eds), *Nation, State and Integration in the Arab World, vol. 2: The Rentier State*, London: Croom Helm, 1987, chs 1–2.
25. See, for example, Anderson, 'The State in the Middle East,' or Giacomo Luciani, 'Economic Foundations of Democracy and Authoritarianism: the Arab World in Comparative Perspective,' *Arab Studies Quarterly*, 10(4), (1988), 457–75.
26. Beblawi and Luciani, 'Introduction,' in *Nation, State*, p. 15.
27. Here I am formalizing the central argument of Beblawi and Luciani, *Nation, State*. A cruder formulation is found in James A. Bill and Robert Springborg's *Politics in the Middle East*, 3rd edn, New York: HarperCollins, 1990, p. 437.
28. See, for example, the cross-regional data in World Bank, *World Development Report, 1987*, pp. 248–9; or in International Monetary Fund, *Government Finance Statistics Yearbook*, vol. 9, 1985, p. 40.
29. Luciani, 'Economic Foundations.'
30. Jill Crystal, 'Coalitions in Monarchies: Kuwait and Qatar,' *Comparative Politics*, 21 (July 1989), 440.
31. Michel Chatelus, 'Policies for Development: Attitudes Toward Industry and Services,' in Beblawi and Luciani, *Nation, State*, p. 112.
32. See, for example, Beblawi in Beblawi and Luciani, *Nation, State*, p. 62.
33. See Delacroix, 'Distributive State' or Mahdavy, 'Patterns and Problems of Economic Development.'
34. Patrick Clawson, 'What's So Good about Stability?' in Henri Barkey (ed.), *The Politics of Economic Reform in the Middle East*, New York: St Martin's Press, 1992, p. 230; Daniel Brumberg, 'Survival Strategies versus Democratic Bargains: the Politics of Economic Reform in Contemporary Egypt,' in ibid., pp. 73–6; Mustapha Said, 'New Face of Authoritarianism.'
35. Clawson, 'What's So Good About Stability?'; and Alan Richards and John Waterbury, *A Political Economy of the Middle East: State, Class and Economic Development*, Boulder, CO: Westview Press, 1990, pp. 436–7.
36. This is true of the most important comparative works on the subject, for example, Richards and Waterbury, *Political Economy of the Middle East*, and Beblawi and Luciani, *Nation, State*. Richards and Waterbury's is a rich and important study; however, it does not develop any formal or systematic theorizing about the relationship between political-electoral forms and economic development in the region. Beblawi *et al.*, develop the 'rentier state' thesis, as described in my introduction. But as I argue here, their central hypothesis is undeveloped and, in many situations, inappropriate or irrelevant. Further, the essays in this work do not use a coherent comparative framework.
37. Much literature emphasizes that these political openings attempted to legitimate and enliven the regimes' development programs. See, for example, Richards and Waterbury, *Political Economy of the Middle East*, p. 437; and Clawson, 'What's So Good About Stability?,' 230.
38. Luciani describes these differences in his 'Allocation and Production States: a Theoretical Framework,' in Beblawi and Luciani, *Nation, State*.
39. O'Donnell and Schmitter, *Transitions from Authoritarian Rule*, pp. 18–20.
40. Barbara Stallings, 'International Influence on Economic Policy: Debt, Stabilization, and Structural Reform,' in Stephen Haggard and Robert Kaufman (eds), *The Politics of Adjustment*, Princeton, NJ: Princeton University Press, 1992, p. 71.
41. Robert Kaufman and Barbara Stallings, 'Introduction,' in their *Debt and Democracy in Latin America*, Boulder, CO: Westview Press, 1989, p. 2.

42. Stephen Haggard and Robert Kaufman, 'The Politics of Stabilization and Adjustment,' in Jeffrey D. Sachs (ed.), *Developing Country Debt and the World Economy*, Chicago: University of Chicago Press, 1989, pp. 267–9.
43. Stallings, 'International Influence.'
44. See my detailed analyses in Chapter 2 of the sources and percentages of exogenous revenues. The distinction between semi- and highly rentier states is made by Mahmud Abdel-fadil in Beblawi and Luciani, *Nation, State*, pp. 83–107; and Luciani, in ibid., 63–82. As they see it, one must distinguish between Middle Eastern states receiving roughly 30 or 40 percent of their revenues from exogenous sources (that is, semi-rentier states) and those receiving over 70 percent of their revenue from such sources (that is, highly rentier states). As my introduction argues, it is in turn worthwhile to identify the distinct political economies of what I call minimally rentier states (that is, those often receiving less than 20 percent of their revenues from exogenous sources).
45. See my detailed analyses in Chapter 2 of the sources and percentages of exogenous revenues.
46. Ibid.
47. O'Donnell and Schmitter, *Transitions from Authoritarian Rule*, p. 9.
48. I. William Zartman, 'Opposition as Support of the State,' in Adeed Dawisha and Zartman (eds), *Beyond Coercion: The Durability of the Arab State* London: Croom Helm, 1987, pp. 77–9.
49. See, for example, Peter Nore and Terisa Turner (eds), *Oil and Class Struggle*, London: Zed Press, 1980; or Karl, 'Petroleum and Political Pacts.'
50. James A. Bill and Robert Springborg, *Politics in the Middle East*, 3rd edn, New York: HarperCollins, 1990, p. 412.
51. World Bank, *World Development Report, 1987*, pp. 248–9.
52. World Bank, *World Development Report, 1986-1993*, tables on central government revenues.
53. Ibid.
54. Karl, 'Petroleum and Political Pacts.'
55. Samuel Huntington, 'The Goals of Development,' in Samuel Huntington and Myron Weiner (eds), *Understanding Political Development*, Boston, MA: Little, Brown, 1987.
56. Karl, 'Dilemmas of Democratization,' 5.

2. The quest for economic heterodoxy in the Middle East*

All Middle Eastern states and societies have felt the effects of neoliberalism, which has become the predominant global economic trend during the past 20 years. But Middle Eastern responses to the new global economic orthodoxy have been varied and inconsistent. This chapter focuses on a critical factor shaping Middle Eastern responses to the seemingly ineluctable advance of neoliberalism: the nature of state access to external capital. I contend that those Middle Eastern states which lacked exogenous resources (including oil and gas revenues and certain kinds of foreign aid) quickly experienced severe fiscal crises and became the 'model' economic reformers of the region. By contrast, I maintain, those states with greater exogenous resources had fiscal crises considerably later (typically in the late 1980s) and those fiscal crises and shortfalls tended to be more ephemeral. Consequently, those states with greater exogenous resources tended to be less beholden to international financial institutions and developed more populist and heterodox responses to their economic problems.

These effects were most pronounced during the 1980s, when many Middle East governments suddenly found it increasingly difficult, if not impossible, to meet their obligations to international donors and creditors. Accordingly, this chapter focuses on these early years of the debt crisis, when exogenous revenues constituted the key factor in determining a regime's approach to reform. These early responses have created legacies and institutions that remain critically important.

BUILDING ON THE ECONOMIC REFORM LITERATURE

Recent scholarship has emphasized that issues of state and regime are critical determinants of the scope and timing of neoliberal economic reforms in the developing world. This approach, by and large, attributes the 'success' and 'failure' of such reforms to the nature of the state and its elite. By contrast, in surveying reformist developments in the Middle East in the 1980s and 1990s, this chapter contends that state access to external capital has been critical in shaping the scope and timing of neoliberal reforms of Third World states.

The perhaps central hypothesis about the success of neoliberal reform focuses on the political and institutional coherence of governing structures. In a leading study, Barbara Stallings and Robert Kaufman contend that the existence of a strong and stable regime, be it democratic or authoritarian, has been a critical factor in the success of orthodox reforms in Latin America. Their survey underscores that the success of economic reform often hinges on the existence of autonomous and cohesive governing structures that control anti-reform social groups. Stallings and Kaufman focus largely on a regime's ability to impose economic austerity on a popular sector that rejects neoliberal reforms.[1] Other studies have argued that economic reforms are often sabotaged by anti-reform capitalists who benefited from statist development policies. Again the problem is an inability of reformist policy-makers to 'insulate' themselves from groups resisting economic reforms.[2]

Scholars also argue that neoliberal reforms often hinge on the state's technical and bureaucratic expertise, and on the regime's alliances with pro-reform private-sector groups. Stallings has argued that governments controlled by 'coalitions with strong internationalist links' have tended to be early and consistent economic reformers. Typically, such internationalist coalitions are dominated by 'sophisticated technocratic teams with extensive foreign training and experience who strongly believe in the value of macroeconomic balance.'[3] Mexico, Thailand, and Korea of the 1980s are examples of the importance of internationalist regime alliances, as Stallings observes.

Here internationalist alliances, as she suggests, provide for the technocratic and educational expertise that are considered essential to the design of a neoliberal reform program. Conversely, regimes lacking such alliances and technocratic expertise presumably tend to be less eager and able to implement economic reforms.[4]

In sum, current development literature focuses on the ability of a state elite to impose neoliberal economic reform on uncooperative or hostile social groups; to forge effective alliances with pro-reform private-sector groups and the international donor and creditor community; and to gather economic intelligence and formulate a coherent reformist strategy.

The availability of 'nonconditional finance' and external capital is an alternative – albeit neglected – explanation of the fact that some Third World states have not implemented substantive neoliberal reforms. Though such an approach has not been used to present a systematic appraisal of the reforms of Third World states, a few analysts have suggested that the availability of exogenous resources has played a critical role in current developments. For example, John Waterbury has argued that Egypt and Turkey had roughly comparable statist development projects in the 1960s and 1970s. But crippling foreign exchange crises compelled Turkey to engage in sweeping neoliberal ʴeforms in the early 1980s. By contrast, Egypt averted such reforms, largely because its considerable exogenous resources (particularly oil revenues and foreign aid) enabled it to maintain its statist and populist projects in the 1980s.[5]

Likewise, Miles Kahler has noted that some states have relied on infusions of external capital to postpone and mitigate their implementation of neoliberal reforms demanded by international donors and creditors. Often, he argues, 'alternative sources of finance' enable Third World countries to avoid – or renege on – IMF or World Bank agreements:

> The availability of nonconditional finance was a disincentive for compliance with IFI [International Financial Institution] conditionality ... By reducing the need for future conditional finance (or even the expectation of such a need), financial windfalls, such as recurrent commodity booms, no-questions-asked aid, or private credit reduces the likelihood of continued cooperation with the IFIs. Typically, the borrower will exploit the conditional lender, agreeing to policy changes only to obtain a seal of approval that will increase its access to other sources of finance.

Kahler argues that Bolivia in the late 1970s and the Philippines in the late 1970s and 1980s exemplify this process of backsliding on agreements with international agencies.[6] But as Waterbury suggests, the availability of unusually large amounts of exogenous resources may well enable a state to preserve the statist development model and to avoid substantive reforms altogether.[7]

Indeed, by building on Waterbury's notion, one can speak volumes about economic (and political) reforms in developing countries. My contention is that Middle Eastern states lacking substantial exogenous resources (especially oil revenues and foreign aid) have experienced severe economic crises and have tended to become serious economic reformers. By contrast, I maintain, those states with greater exogenous resources have often had milder economic crises and have typically developed more populist development models. Windfalls such as oil revenues and foreign aid are important in the development process, because they enable developing countries to avoid or mitigate dependence on the conditional finance of the IMF and World Bank.

The following section uses a resource-based model to illuminate a central development trajectory in the Middle East in the 1980s and 1990s. I focus on the cases of Morocco, Turkey, Egypt, and Kuwait, though I also refer to other important regional developments. I am particularly interested in state access to various forms of external capital, or what scholars of the Middle East usually call exogenous revenues. These 'rents' – for example, bank loans, oil revenues, and foreign aid – accrue directly to the state, and account for almost all of the foreign exchange flows in the Middle East. In the early and middle 1980s – the first years of the Third World debt crisis – such flows were critical in determining the scope and timing of the adoption of neoliberal reform.

A WORD ABOUT THE IMPACT OF EXOGENOUS REVENUES ON STATE DEVELOPMENT POLICIES: THE QUEST FOR POPULISM

In the 1950s and 1960s, relatively resource-poor Middle Eastern countries relied on foreign aid and bank loans to finance the development of coercive and distributive bureaucracies. Broadly speaking, the origin of expansive policies in those states outside the Gulf was in the application or reinterpretation of the Nasirist model of 'Arab socialism.' Here of course the Nasirist model reflected the drive toward statist economic development occurring throughout the Third World during the postwar era. But distinguishing the development of state welfare and intervention in the Middle East was its extraordinary dependence on external sources, especially during the 1970s.[8]

After the 1973 Arab–Israeli War, oil prices quadrupled and foreign aid flows within and into the region increased dramatically. These exogenous revenues funded a massive expansion of the distributive policies and bureaucracies of the 'oil-poor' Arab states, including Morocco, Tunisia, Egypt, Syria, and Jordan. Thus, despite their putative ideological differences, regimes in these countries sought to augment the state's role in the economy: greatly expanding their budgets, infrastructures, subsidies, social services, and public sectors. 'Ideologies vary,' observe Richards and Waterbury of the expansionary 1970s, 'but not the perceived need for state intervention.'[9]

Of course, the composition of the ruling coalitions varied markedly from country to country. Relatively broad and inclusive ruling coalitions in Egypt and Tunisia, for example, contrasted sharply with the narrow sectarian base of the Syrian regime; and with the traditional Beduin orientation of the Jordanian monarchy. But in the 1970s, the thrust of economic development in all these countries was toward a dynamic expansion of state intervention in the economy, and a sharp increase in consumptive and distributive policies, as fueled by exogenous revenues.[10]

Consequently, the region's liberal monarchies 'possess public sectors of a size and weight equal to those of the "socialist" countries.'[11] Here the exogenous revenues of the 1970s consolidated two region-wide processes: first, the expansion of the state's control over the economy; and second, a marked increase in the state's ability to use distributive policies to ameliorate political conflict. In short, such 'intense statism' characterized regimes espousing both 'Arab socialism' and 'laissez-faire' monarchism in the 1970s, as Kiren Aziz Chaudhry argues.[12]

In sum, in the 1970s and the early 1980s, oil-related wealth and other kinds of foreign aid preserved and in important respects enhanced the distributive and interventionist capacities of relatively rent-poor Middle Eastern states.

These exogenous revenues did what all such revenues tend to do, other things being equal: enhance and preserve forms of populist consumption and distributive bureaucracies. In all cases, exogenous revenues freed the states from many of the burdens of direct taxation. In turn, existing regimes were able to ameliorate political conflict through their distribution of patronage, and to secure the political acquiescence of their populations through their provision of social welfare.

Consequently, authoritarian rule became more durable in the Arab world, as the massive exogenous revenues of the 1970s worked to stabilize regimes. Different analysts observe how this dynamic was played out in particular cases and systematically in countries throughout the region.[13] Further, scholars working with the rentier state paradigm show how exogenous revenues enabled the relatively poor Arab countries to sustain their statist projects. Waterbury, for example, notes that exogenous windfalls of the 1970s and early 1980s enabled the regime of Sadat and Mubarak to preserve and develop in certain respects, the Nasirist social contract.[14]

In sum, Middle Eastern rulers have tended, whenever possible, to use significant exogenous revenues to pursue distributive economic policies. The oil monarchies have pursued an optimal development strategy, one that the other regional states attempted to replicate in the 1970s, albeit to a lesser degree. In the 1980s and 1990s, the relatively rent-poor states turned reluctantly to austerity and neoliberal orthodoxy, only after the evaporation of their exogenous resources worked to trigger severe budgetary gaps. Thus, while exogenous windfalls tended to strengthen regional regimes in the 1970s and early 1980s, drops in these revenues tended to destabilize the regimes in the middle and late 1980s.

EXOGENOUS REVENUES AND THE ERA OF NEOLIBERAL REFORM IN THE MIDDLE EAST

This section describes how levels of exogenous revenues have patterned the process of economic crisis, stabilization, and reform in Middle Eastern countries in the 1980s and 1990s. It focuses on Turkey, Morocco, Egypt, and Kuwait, though it also briefly reviews developments in other Middle Eastern countries.

My conceptualization of state access to exogenous revenues in the early 1980s is presented in Tables 2.1–2.4, which also serve as the bases for the typology of Middle Eastern political development that I present in the subsequent chapters. With some modifications, I measure that access using an approach developed by World Bank analysts and by scholars working with the rentier state paradigm. Quite simply, that approach examines the level of

Table 2.1   Turkey (US$ bn)

	1979	1980	1981	1982	1983	1984
Current government revenues (includes grants but not loans)	15.98	12.43	12.99	10.68	10.21	—
Total borrowing	4.40	2.12	1.05	—	—	—
Total revenues	20.38	14.54	14.04	14.00	13.10	13.40
Exogenous revenues						
Grants (mostly US)	0.01	0.08	0.14	0.26	0.30	0.20
Mineral extraction (including oil)	0.60	0.60	0.60	0.60	0.60	0.60
Oil pipeline fees	0.10	0.10	0.10	0.10	0.10	0.10
Borrowing minus repayment	0.75	0.01	0.33	—	0.01	0
Total	1.46	0.79	1.17	0.96	1.01	0.90
Exogenous resources as % of total revenues	7	5	8	7	8	7
Additional exogenous resources						
Expatriate labor remittances	1.80	2.20	2.60	2.20	1.50	1.90

Sources: Revenues and borrowing, except total revenues 1982–4: IMF, *International Financial Statistics Yearbook*, November–December 1986, p. 186; 1982–4 figures: *Middle East Economic Digest*, September 30, 1983, p. 48. Mineral and oil revenues: various *Economist Intelligence Unit* country reports, 1982–4. Pipeline estimate: *Economist Intelligence Unit, Report No. 4, 1990*, p. 17. Grant aid: *Statistical Annex to the Annual Development Committee Report to Congress*, 1985, p. 29. Labor remittances: IMF as cited in A. Richards and J. Waterbury, *A Political Economy of the Middle East*, Boulder, CO: Westview Press, 1990, p. 390.

exogenous resources as a percentage of total economic resources. Some analysts prefer to measure exogenous revenues as a percentage of state revenues; others assess the role of exogenous resources in the economy as a whole. Following the approach of several contributors to *The Rentier State* volume,[15] I measure the variable of rentier resources in relation to total state revenues (and not in relation to GDP). I focus on state resources, as my primary concern is the state's policy-making autonomy: that is, its ability to maintain heterodox macroeconomic policies.

Here I follow a strand in the literature that considers, for example, expatriate labor remittances and tourist-generated revenues to be quasi-rent and not 'pure' rent. Such revenues depend on labor and taxation, and by and

Table 2.2   Morocco (US$ bn)

	1979	1980	1981	1982	1983	1984
Central government revenues (includes grants but not loans)	3.99	4.37	3.88	4.00	3.40	2.99
Total borrowing	1.48	1.86	2.18	1.61	1.47	1.50[a]
Total government revenues	5.47	6.23	6.06	5.61	4.87	4.49
Exogenous revenues						
Grants (mostly Saudi)	1.25	1.25	1.25	0.50	0.40	0.40
Phosphates	0.49	0.60	0.74	0.49	0.34	0.49
Borrowing minus repayment	0.04	0.04	0.01	0.03	0.02	—
Total	1.78	1.89	2.00	1.02	0.66	0.79
Total exogenous revenues as % of total revenues	32	30	33	18	14	18
Additional external resources						
Free oil (Saudi)	—	—	—	—	—	0.80
Expatriate labor remittances	0.39	1.00	1.00	0.84	0.89	0.85

Note: [a] Estimated.

Sources: Revenues, borrowings, and phosphates: IMF, *International Financial Statistics Yearbook*, November–December 1986, p. 350, and December 1985, pp. 334–5. Grants: I. William Zartman (ed.), *The Political Economy of Morocco*, New York: Praeger, 1987, pp. 198–9 and *Middle East Economic Digest*, September 2, 1983. Free Saudi oil: Zartman, ibid. Labor remittances: A. Richards and J. Waterbury, *A Political Economy of the Middle East*, Boulder, CO: Westview Press, 1990.

large are earned and held privately. On the one hand, these revenues are valuable sources of foreign currency, and often help to maintain a socio-economic equilibrium – or a 'rentier society,' as some observers have it.[16] My approach, in sum, accepts the notion that drops in such income increase pressure on the state, especially in its dealings with Western creditors and its design of a development program. Expatriate labor remittances are especially important in this regard, and I have noted their levels in the tables. Moreover, I am careful to note the importance of quasi-rents in my consideration of the Moroccan, Turkish, and Egyptian cases.

Table 2.3   Egypt (US$ bn)

	1981	1982	1983	1984
Central government revenues (includes grants but not loans)	10.70	11.26	12.46	12.85
Total borrowing	1.48	4.39	2.75	2.83
Total government revenues	12.18	15.65	15.21	15.68
Exogenous resources				
Grants (US)	0.79	1.01	1.19	1.33
Oil revenues	3.18	3.3	2.8	2.23
Suez Canal revenues	0.78	0.91	0.97	1.00
Borrowing minus repayment	0.95	2.07	2.61	2.10
Total	6.36	7.73	7.83	6.78
Exogenous revenues as % of total revenues	52	49	51	43
Additional exogenous resources				
Value of domestic oil resources used in Egypt	2.50	2.50	2.50	2.50
Expatriate labor remittances	2.20	2.50	3.70	4.00

Sources: Government revenues, borrowing, and Suez Canal revenues: IMF, *International Financial Statistics Yearbook*, November–December 1986, p. 198. Grants: *Statistical Annex to Annual Development Committee Report to Congress*, 1985, p. 13. 1981–4 oil revenues: *Meri Report: Egypt*, London: Croom Helm, 1985, p. 121, and *Middle East Economic Digest*, April 1, 1983, p. 12. Domestic oil resources: A. Richards and J. Waterbury, *A Political Economy of the Middle East*, Boulder, CO: Westview Press, 1990, p. 234. Labor remittances: IMF as cited in Richards and Waterbury, ibid., p. 390.

On the other hand, such revenues typically by-pass the state. To claim some of these resources for itself, the state must extract them through some form of taxation. In theory, therefore, they do not increase, and may even erode, its autonomy and its ability to implement a development program. Consequently, I have excluded these quasi-rents from the formulation of economic-policy categories in the tables. Equally important, in all four cases, most external capital is in fact exogenous rent flowing directly to the state.

My overriding interest is the state's access to foreign exchange, which has dictated the magnitude and timing of economic reforms in countries throughout the Middle East. States lacking hard currency (namely, Turkey and Morocco) had no choice but to turn to the IMF and World Bank and to impose

Table 2.4   Kuwait (US$ bn)

	1979–80	1980–1	1981–2	1982–3	1983–4
Government revenues	23.61	21.67	14.60	16.40	15.82
of which:					
Oil and gas	20.31	15.19	9.50	10.13	9.50
Investment income	3.00	5.95	4.66	5.45	5.42
Other (fees, etc.)	0.30	0.53	0.44	0.82	0.90
Expenditure	8.11	9.82	12.67	13.54	12.62
Budget surplus	15.50	11.85	1.93	2.86	3.20
Exogenous revenues as % of total revenues	99	98	97	95	94

Source: IMF Survey of Kuwaiti Finance Ministry data, reported in *Middle East Economic Digest*, August 26, 1983.

(official) stabilization and austerity programs, in the early part of the decade. By contrast, those regional states with substantial exogenous resources had foreign exchange flows that enabled them to postpone implementation of economic reform. American grant aid was an insignificant component of government income in the late 1970s and early 1980s. Expatriate labor remittances (in relation to the size of the economy) were considerably smaller than were Egyptian and Moroccan remittances. As well, Turkey's oil resources have been relatively insignificant, covering only 15 percent of domestic oil consumption. Petroleum and its derivatives constituted 75 percent of Turkish imports in the early 1980s.[17]

Though its economy began to decline in 1977, Morocco had access to significant exogenous revenues, mainly in the form of foreign aid from Saudi Arabia and other Gulf countries, until 1981. Saudi largesse was in fact a direct and critical support of the Moroccan war effort in the Western Sahara, which reportedly cost the government approximately $1 billion per year during the late 1970s and early 1980s.[18] But by 1982, with the sharp downturn in oil prices and the faltering of negotiations over the Western Sahara, Saudi Arabia slashed its aid to Morocco. By 1983, Saudi giving was thought to be but one-third of its 1979–81 level.[19] Meanwhile, the war in the Western Sahara continued apace; and phosphate income (the state's only other significant exogenous resource) also declined sharply from its 1981 level. Thus, while foreign aid and phosphate revenues roughly equaled one-third of total government revenues in 1981, these two sources were the equivalent of only one-sixth of total revenues in 1983 and 1984. Finally, though massive bank loans had spurred rapid economic expansion during 1973–7, Morocco's net resources from borrowing were negligible in the early 1980s. In fact, the furious borrowings of the middle and late 1970s had translated into a crushing debt in the early 1980s. Consequently, most of the borrowings of the early 1980s were used to finance debt payments; in 1983, for example, debt service claimed $3 billion.[20] In turn, this steep decline in exogenous revenues contributed to the foreign exchange crisis that compelled Morocco to enter into an official stabilization agreement with the IMF in 1983.

While Morocco and Turkey flirted with economic collapse, Egypt was awash in foreign exchange and experiencing rapid growth in the early 1980s.[21] Here oil resources constituted a key difference between semi-rentier Egypt and minimally rentier Turkey and Morocco. The bulk of Moroccan and Turkish hard currency was used to finance oil imports. Morocco spent roughly $1 billion per annum on oil imports in the early 1980s; and Turkey's annual oil import bill averaged roughly $3 billion in the same period.[22] By contrast, Egypt imported almost little oil in the early 1980s: of its 38 million tons in total annual oil production, roughly 20 million tons were consumed domestically.[23] The value of this consumption is estimated to have been as high as $3 billion per annum,[24] which of course represents a critical saving in foreign exchange. Further, annual Egyptian oil income averaged about $2.8 billion in the early 1980s.[25] Thus, altogether the total value of Egyptian oil production is sometimes estimated to be approximately $6 billion. Consequently, the (second) oil shock of 1979–80 generated an unprecedented windfall for Egypt (as oil export revenues reportedly surged to $4.5 billion in 1980) – and, at the same time, worked to undermine the Moroccan and Turkish economies.[25]

Oil aside, Egypt had additional exogenous resources that Turkey and Morocco either lacked altogether or had in lesser quantities. Concerning locational rents, Suez Canal revenues annually earned Egypt almost $1 billion in hard currency; whereas an Iraqi pipeline produced insignificant revenues for Turkey in the early 1980s, and Morocco did not enjoy any revenues from such strategically placed pipelines or canals. In the early 1980s, and unlike the situation in Turkey and Morocco, Egyptian net borrowing still represented an important influx of revenues. Finally, US aid to Egypt greatly outstripped US aid to Turkey and, after 1981, proved to be much more reliable and significant than Saudi aid to Morocco. (Annual US grants to Egypt exceeded $2 billion by 1985.[26])

Though Kuwaiti revenues dropped precipitously between 1979–80 and 1983–4, Kuwaiti expenditures increased dramatically during these years. Much of that increase in expenditure financed the dramatic expansion of social welfare projects and other consumptive policies. Here one should note that the increase in consumptive policies and social spending in Egypt in the early 1980s was closely linked to the upsurge in its exogenous revenues. By contrast, the great increase in Kuwaiti social spending was entirely divorced from vagaries in state revenue. More broadly, the Kuwaiti case indicates that such highly rentier states (that is, the Arabian oil monarchies) have been unique in not needing to grapple with the conventional formulations of economic orthodoxy and austerity.

EARLY VERSUS LATE ECONOMIC REFORM: THE MIDDLE EAST IN GLOBAL PERSPECTIVE

Recent global economic trends have pushed all Middle Eastern regimes to grapple with economic reforms. The speed, breadth, and consistency of the reforms are what tend to distinguish those states lacking significant exogenous resources from those states commanding such resources. In a word, access to exogenous revenues roughly conditions the nature and timing of Middle Eastern economic reform. As argued in the following paragraphs, my approach provides a rough typology of the economic reform process in Middle Eastern states. That typology builds on Barbara Stallings' notions of 'early' and 'late' reformers, conceptualizations developed in her survey of economic reform in 15 African, East Asian, and Latin American countries. Most relevant for my purposes is her periodization of economic stabilization, as most Middle Eastern governments have focused their reform efforts on that process (as opposed to structural adjustment)[27].

The 15 countries do not constitute a scientific sampling, though they did include cases that demonstrated highly variable responses to economic crisis and to demands for reform from international donors and creditors. The first category includes the 'early stabilizers': Mexico, Thailand, Korea, and Costa Rica. In response to economic shock, these governments took the initiative in the implementation of stabilization during 1980-2. 'Middle stabilizers' include the Philippines, Ghana, Jamaica, and the Dominican Republic, which stabilized in 1983-4, but mainly in response to intense pressure from international agencies, particularly the IMF and USAID.

For most of the other countries, writes Stallings, 'stabilization was yet more controversial and did not take place until the economic situation had further deteriorated later in the decade.'[28] The 'late stabilizers' include the special case of Chile,[29] Colombia, and Nigeria, which undertook reform between 1985 and 1988. The 'late-late stabilizers' – Argentina, Brazil, and Peru – implemented some manner of orthodox stabilization in 1989-90, after their heterodox stabilization attempts of 1985-6 had failed. Stallings also calls Zambia a 'late-late stabilizer,' though the Kaunda government was unable to maintain any consistent economic strategy during the 1980s.[30]

Stallings observes that most of the governments' responses to the international economic shocks of the 1980s fell into three categories. In the early and successful stabilizers (including Korea, Thailand, Chile, and Mexico), the regimes and the private-sector elites tended to concur that their interests lay in rapid and dynamic orthodox reform. Needing little prompting from international agencies, and possessing sufficient technical expertise, these states 'had the political capacity, through various forms of authoritarian governing structures, to implement their chosen policies.'[31]

The second group includes the African and less-developed Latin American nations, which had low technical capacities and were compelled by international actors to undertake reform. The third group includes transitional democracies (Brazil, Argentina, and the Philippines) which were unable to implement consistent stabilization policies. They had the technical capacity, but lacked the highly institutionalized state structures that were necessary for the imposition of far-reaching economic reform.

Cutting across these trajectories, and bringing stabilization to the fore of the Third World policy agenda, were international economic shocks. In particular, the global recession and the precipitous decline in lending meant that developing countries with inefficient import-substitution models faced severe foreign-exchange crises. Above all, regimes throughout the Third World had to impose orthodoxy to obtain resources that were critical to their stability.

Scholars note that the Middle Eastern political economy is unique, largely because most of the major states of the region receive unusually high levels of exogenous revenues. Above all, these revenues tend to delay and mitigate the state resource gaps and foreign exchange crises that compel Middle Eastern countries to undertake economic reform and to reach accommodations with international creditors and donors. I would argue as well that *substantial levels* of exogenous revenues function in a similar manner in other world regions. But in the Middle East the unusual prominence of such resources has created a regional development pattern, one that has shaped the economic reforms of relatively autonomous authoritarian regimes. Thus, as I argue below, whereas Stallings and others point to issues of state, regime, and opposition as being important to global trends in the implementation of economic reform, exogenous revenues have contributed to a distinctive reformist pattern in the Middle East.

Of course, inefficient development models and changing global economic forces have compelled all Middle Eastern states (except the oil monarchies) to undertake far-reaching neoliberal reforms. Obviously, a range of economic and political factors shape the process. But, as I argue below, a critical element in the timing, nature and scope of Middle Eastern reforms has been the availability of exogenous resources.

In receiving the lowest levels of exogenous revenues, Turkey was the first and most serious implementer of official neoliberal reform (1980). Morocco, as the other low-rent state in the Middle East, followed soon thereafter (1983). International economic shocks caused both the Turkish and the Moroccan economy to slip into crises of debt and foreign exchange; though in the case of the latter, Saudi foreign aid appears to have delayed and mitigated the crisis somewhat. In sum, the two archetypal minimally rentier states were 'model' reformers, as they began the process earlier than the other Middle Eastern regimes, implemented the reforms for extended periods, and achieved far-reaching goals. The Turkish military regime (1980–4) imposed the reforms with brutal efficiency. Ozal's subsequent administration followed through on critical restructuring projects. Though turning to increasingly expansionary policies in the middle and late 1980s to improve its electoral fortunes, the Motherland Party did oversee the completion of the most substantive economic restructuring in the Middle East. Likewise, throughout the 1980s and 1990s, Morocco consistently maintained and implemented orthodox policies (including some privatization). Thus, in the 1990s, the World Bank deemed Morocco a model reformer.

It seems that Turkey and Morocco were the first regional states to begin orthodox stabilization, largely because they were the first states to run out of resources and to experience crises. Like Stalling's 'early stabilizers,' both states relied on highly institutionalized and authoritarian structures during the critical years of implementation of reform. Also, as in the early stabilizers, a particularly skilled and cohesive technocratic elite pushed and designed Turkish reforms. But why did officially sanctioned Moroccan reforms precede comparable ones in, for example, Tunisia (1986), Jordan (1989), and Egypt (1991)? For these other regimes do not seem to have been less institutionalized or to have possessed lesser technical skills, than did the Moroccan regime.

Here a critical factor seems to be exogenous resources. As I describe below, Tunisia has commanded more exogenous resources than have Morocco and Turkey, with oil revenues equaling roughly one-quarter of state income during the early and mid-1980s.[32] Accordingly, official Tunisian reforms were postponed until after the collapse in oil prices in 1985. Similarly, the collapse of foreign aid receipts in the late 1980s, which had underwritten at least half of the state budget earlier in the decade, forced Jordan to find an accommodation with the international agencies.[33] Since Jordanian access remained low through the 1990s – dropping to just 14 percent of the state budget by 1993[34] – Jordan has had no choice but to adhere to strict orthodox stabilization measures.

Exogenous resources allowed Egypt to postpone its substantive official reform program until the early 1990s. Then declining exogenous resources had increased the regime's reformist inclinations in the late 1980s. But since its sources of exogenous income were more diversified than were those of Jordan and Tunisia, Egypt was able to evade reforms until the 1990s. But even then, the Egyptian path to substantive orthodoxy was unusual: *before* the onset of full-blown economic crisis, and because of geopolitics, Egypt received an unprecedented offer of financial assistance from Western and Arab powers in the early 1990s. In a word, Egypt agreed to implement orthodox policies in order to receive roughly $5 billion per annum in aid (the most received by any country in the world). Thus, exogenous resources conditioned the Egyptian stance toward reform throughout the 1980s and early 1990s.[35]

In sum, Egypt, Jordan, and to a lesser extent Tunisia were 'late' reformers, because of their substantive exogenous resources. In the 1990s, however, these relatively resource-poor countries refrained from reversing, and indeed consistently maintained, their austerity and stabilization programs. Late and inconsistent reformers include Iran (early 1990s), Iraq (late 1980s), and Algeria (late 1980s). These states commanded greater exogenous resources (as a percentage of state revenues) than did Egypt, Jordan, and Tunisia throughout the 1980s. The collapse of Algeria's oil and gas revenues in the late 1980s prompted its serious (though largely unofficial) stabilization program. As well, declining oil prices spurred Iraq's unofficial reforms during 1987-9 and Iran's unofficial reforms in the 1990s; however, a more direct cause of Iraqi and Iranian economic troubles was the overwhelming costs of war reconstruction. (Estimates of Iraqi reconstruction costs, for example, were $230 billion in 1988.[36])

Still, both Iran and Algeria reversed their drives toward orthodoxy, with the former reinstating highly heterodox policies in the spring of 1994, and the latter returning to expansionary policies in 1992. Though having some initial successes in the privatization of the state agricultural sector, the Iraqi reform program was a dramatic failure and was abandoned by 1990. Thus, in the regional context and in accord with their impressive exogenous resources, these countries have been 'late-late' and highly inconsistent reformers.

At the end of the 1990s, access to exogenous revenues still conditions the overriding development trends in the Middle East. Arab countries receiving high marks from the IMF - Morocco, Tunisia, Jordan, and Egypt[37] - tended to be those commanding the lowest levels of nonconditional finance. The key exception here seems to be Egypt. But, as was argued above, access to unprecedented levels of foreign aid dictated the Egyptian embrace of neoliberalism in the 1990s, as the Egyptian government used its unique geopolitical position to bargain for unprecedented assistance from Western and Gulf powers.

Beyond the special case of Egypt, the predominant trend has divided the region into relatively rent-poor reformers and relatively rent-poor laggards: to wit, those countries maintaining the most heterodox policies are of course the highly rentier oil monarchies. Though declining oil revenues have prompted these states to promote the private sector and scale back some of their expenditures, their version of reform and austerity is of a different magnitude altogether. Despite declining oil revenues, highly rentier states such as Saudi Arabia and Kuwait have not made serious efforts to introduce even rudimentary personal taxation systems in recent years, or to roll back 'the world's most generous welfare states.'[38] That reluctance exemplifies a general tendency among Middle Eastern states in recent decades to opt for populist statecraft whenever, and to the greatest extent, possible.

NOTES

* This chapter is based on my article 'External Capital and Political Liberalizations: A Typology of Middle Eastern Development in the 1980s and 1990s,' *Journal of International Affairs*, 49(1) (Summer 1995).

1. Robert Kaufman and Barbara Stallings (eds), *Debt and Democracy in Latin America*, Boulder, CO: Westview Press, 1989, pp. 208–9.
2. See, for example, Henri Barkey, 'State Autonomy and the Crisis of Import Substitution,' *Comparative Political Studies*, 2(3) (1989), 291–314.
3. Barbara Stallings, 'International Influence on Economic Policy: Debt, Stabilization and the Crisis of Import Substitution,' in Stephan Haggard and Robert Kaufman (eds), *The Politics of Economic Adjustment*, Princeton, NJ: Princeton University Press, 1992, p. 75.
4. John Waterbury, 'The Political Management of Economic Adjustment and Reform,' in his *Politics of Public Sector Reform and Privatization*, Boulder, CO: Westview Press, 1990, p. 49.
5. Ibid.
6. Miles Kahler, 'External Influence, Conditionality, and the Politics of Adjustment,' in Haggard and Kaufman, *Politics of Economic Adjustment*, p. 111.
7. Waterbury, 'The Political Management of Economic Adjustment,' p. 49. See, for example, Hazem Beblawi, 'The Rentier State in the Arab World,' in H. Beblawi and G. Luciani (eds), *The Rentier State*, London: Croom Helm, 1987; Alan Richards and John Waterbury, *Political Economy of the Middle East: State, Class and Economic Development*, Boulder, CO: Westview Press, 1990; p. 238.
8. Kiren Aziz Chaudhry, 'Economic Liberalization and the Lineages of the Rentier State,' *Comparative Politics*, 27 (October 1994), 51.
9. Richards and Waterbury, *Political Economy of the Middle East*, p. 238.
10. See, for example, F. Gregory Gause, 'Revolutionary Fevers and Revolutionary Contagion: Domestic Structures and the "Export" of Revolution in the Middle East,' *Journal of South Asian and Middle Eastern Studies*, 14(3) (Spring 1991), 1–23.
11. Chaudhry, 'Economic Liberalization,' p. 51.
12. Ibid.
13. See, for example, Gause, 'Revolutionary Fevers,' or Chaudhry, 'Economic Liberalization.'
14. John Waterbury, 'The "Soft State" and the Open Door: Egypt's Experience with Economic Liberalization, 1974–1984,' *Comparative Politics*, 18(1) (October 1985), 65–84.
15. See, for example, Beblawi's approach in 'The Rentier State in the Arab World,' in Beblawi and Luciani, *Rentier State*.
16. See Thomas Stauffer's 'Income Measurement in Arab States,' in Beblawi and Luciani, *Rentier State*, pp. 22–48.
17. Middle East Research Institute of the University of Pennsylvania, *MERI Report: Turkey*, London: Croom Helm, 1985, p. 79.

18. John Damis, *Conflict in Northwest Africa: The Western Sahara Dispute*, Stanford, CA: Hoover Institution Press, 1983, p. 134.
19. Richard Pomfret, 'Morocco's International Economic Relations,' in William Zartman (ed.), *The Political Economy of Morocco*, New York: Praeger, 1987, p. 199.
20. Ibid.
21. See, for example, 'While the Sun Shines, Egypt Knocks Holes in the Roof,' and 'Cash on the Nile,' *The Economist*, April 1, 1984.
22. See *Middle East Economic Digest*, August 12, 1983, 39; and MERI: *Turkey*, 79.
23. *Middle East Economic Digest*, November 4, 1983, 5.
24. Ibid. See, for example, the Egypt report in the *Middle East Economic Digest*, January 20, 1984.
25. Richards and Waterbury, *Political Economy of the Middle East*, p. 233. See the detailed breakdown of oil revenues in MERI Report: *Egypt*, London: Croom Helm, 1985, pp. 95–7, 172–9.
26. See data on aid to Egypt in the *Statistical Annex to the Annual Development Committee Report to Congress, 1985–89*, Washington, DC: US Government Printing Office.
27. Stabilization tends to refer to orthodox measures – including devaluations, budget deficit reduction, credit restrictions, and restraining or lowering wages – that fight inflation and ease balance-of-payment deficits. Stabilization tends to be the most politicized aspect of economic reform in the Middle East and elsewhere.
28. Barbara Stallings, 'International Influence on Economic Policy: Debt, Stabilization, and Structural Reform,' in Stephan Haggard and Robert Kaufman (eds), *The Politics of Adjustment*, Princeton, NJ: Princeton University Press, 1992, p. 74.
29. Having maintained stringent orthodoxy between 1973 and 1981, Chile implemented more expansionary policies between 1981 and 1985. Still, on the whole, the Pinochet regime engineered perhaps the most rigorous neoliberal model in the Third World.
30. Stallings, 'International Influence,' p. 71.
31. Ibid.
32. The Economist Intelligence Unit, *Country Profile: Tunisia*, London: The Economist Intelligence Unit, 1986, p. 20.
33. Robert Satloff, 'Jordan's Great Gamble: Economic Crisis and Political Reform,' in Henri J. Barkey (ed.), *The Politics of Economic Reform in the Middle East*, New York: St Martin's Press, 1992, p. 130.
34. The Economist Intelligence Unit, *Jordan Country Profile, 1994–95*, London: The Economist Intelligence Unit, p. 28.
35. William Schmidt, 'A Deluge of Foreign Assistance Fails to Revive Egypt's Stricken Economy,' *New York Times*, October 17, 1993.
36. Lawrence Freedman and Efrain Karsh, *The Gulf Conflict, 1990–91*, Princeton, NJ: Princeton University Press, 1993, p. 39.
37. Karen Pfeifer, 'How Tunisia, Morocco, Jordan and Even Egypt Became IMF "Success Stories" in the 1990s,' *Middle East Report*, Spring 1999, 23–7.
38. James A. Bill and Robert Springborg, *Politics in the Middle East*, 3rd edn, New York: HarperCollins, 1990, pp. 79–80, 430.

3. The relationship between economic and political development in the Middle East: a narrative political economy

This chapter analyzes the relationship between electoral forms and economic pressures in Middle Eastern countries representing three distinct political economies. Its primary concern is the effect of economic resources on authoritarian regimes designing and controlling processes of political liberalization, democratization, and redemocratization. Chapter 4 closely compares the electoral design and the parliamentary role of bourgeois groups in the four cases. This chapter introduces and narrates the contemporary political economies of the four cases. It seeks to explicate the relationship between economic and political variables: to flesh out the impact of economic resources on political development. It assumes the form of a broad causal sketch, one that will be embellished and explicated in the subsequent chapter. The first two sections argue that, despite their differences in regime types, the Turkish and Moroccan cases share important commonalities as minimally rentier states. The next two sections contend that exogenous resources enabled Egypt and Kuwait to maintain comparatively populist policies and alliances.

TURKEY: REDEMOCRATIZATION IN A MINIMALLY RENTIER STATE

The September 1980 coup marked the beginning of the transformation of Turkey's political and economic life. It signalled a move from an ISI-based economy to a comparatively open, orthodox and export-oriented one; and at the same time, it initiated an institutional and constitutional restructuring of the Turkish political system.

Scholars note that the 1980 military takeover, unlike the previous ones, attempted to effect social transformations. The import and permanence of that new social 'hegemony' are the subject of debate.[1] But none denies that the coup initiated a new era in the Turkish political economy.

An import-substitution program had dominated the Turkish economy during the postwar era, and had generated rapid growth until the second half of the 1970s. During this period, exports were confined to primary products and comprised a small percentage of GNP; and workers' remittances and borrowing spurred economic growth. Like the Latin American ISI models, the Turkish program was unable to extend import substitution to capital goods industries, as increasingly expensive import inputs undermined domestic production and investment. The Turkish model was particularly inflexible in that it used extraordinary protectionist measures, did not seek to achieve any balance between import substitution and export promotion, and did not subject even mature industries to competition from abroad.[2] Consequently, rising import bills pushed the Turkish economy into crisis during the late 1970s: inflation accelerated, the balance of payments became critical, and GNP growth dropped precipitously.[3] By 1977, external shocks and the worsening balance of payments had generated a debt crisis and severe shortages of basic consumer goods.

A lack of state autonomy and deficiencies in the ISI model led to the near-collapse of the Turkish economy in the late 1970s. Generally speaking, the 'rent-seeking' behavior among firms and business groups seeking advantages within the import-substition regime had come to cripple the state's economic policy. That is, the government's dispensing of subsidies, foreign credit, and import licences generated intense competition among business groups seeking profitable niches within a heavily protected domestic market. By early 1980, amid economic and political crisis, almost all private sector groups were calling for the implementation of an orthodox reform package, and were searching for advantageous positions in the developing export-promotion regime. But their rent-seeking behavior during the 1970s and the weakness of the state had helped to induce the crisis and the subsequent coup.[4]

More broadly, ISI had supported industries that were unable to compete internationally, and had created a large and inefficient public sector that ultimately produced crippling levels of inflation. By 1980, the GDP growth rate fell to −0.7 percent and the rate of inflation reached 110.2 percent, its highest level ever.[5] Above all, Turkey faced an unbridgeable foreign exchange crisis. In turn, an insolvent Turkish state had no choice but to consider the radical orthodox reforms demanded by international donors and the private sector.

At the same time, Turkey's fragmented and paralyzed parliament reached a deadlock over a range of critical issues, including economics, foreign policy, and the election of a new president. Political violence and labor unrest, in turn, rose to unprecedented levels. On September 12, the military intervened: dissolving parliament, suspending civilian institutions, and signalling to the IMF and World Bank its intention to implement an orthodox reform program.[6]

Barkey observes that the incoming Turkish military regime, led by General

Kenan Evren, sought to 'engineer'[7] a traditional bureaucratic-authoritarian political-economic transformation (though it did not, Barkey notes, pursue the objective of 'industrial deepening'). The military's structural adjustment program had been formulated by the center-right government of Suleyman Demirel in January of 1980, but had been vigorously opposed by the working class and opposition political parties.

A central aim of the military intervention was a diminution or elimination of the main redistributive and statist policies of the ISI era. The junta sought the privatization of much of the state sector; the reduction of inflation, budget deficits, and subsidies; the deregulation of the exchange rate; the removal of price controls on state economic enterprises; the removal of tariff and nontariff barriers; the internationalization of the Turkish economy through the 48 per cent devaluation of the Turkish lira against the dollar; and large price increases for goods produced by the public sector. In purging the opposition, the military regime was able to implement these measures in a rapid and dynamic fashion.[8] The country, observers maintained in the early and mid-1980s, had become an 'IMF showcase.'[9]

At the heart of the economic restructuring effort, as advanced by the junta, were plans to reinvigorate a moribund export sector. Here the imposition of austerity on the popular sectors, including increases in unemployment and the decline of real wages, was crucial. 'One of the most distinguishing characteristics of the early 1980s,' notes Ziya Onis, 'concerned the imposition of a compulsory incomes policy that resulted in a decisive shift in income distribution away from wage earners.'[10] A central component of the process was the regime's exclusion of the labor movement from the formulation of policy. Naturally, the military eliminated the right to strike.[11] Further, the military's labor legislation forbade unionizing among civil service workers.[12]

Such coercion was but one factor in the military's successful implementation of economic reform. Support for the military's stabilization and reform of the economy came from the urban middle classes, who appreciated the regime's ability to ensure political stability and to end the shortage of basic consumer goods. As well, powerful new financial groupings associated with Ozal and his team of technocrats rallied round the military's implementation of economic reform. Such interests, by and large, sought to benefit from new types of export promotion, and were linked to multinational corporations and internationalized segments of the banking sector.[13] The military's reorganization of the political system enabled these groupings to reach political maturity in the post-1983 era, as I explain below.

The Coup and the Bourgeoisie

Initially, the Turkish bourgeoisie was enthusiastic about the military takeover and the military's implementation of stabilization and reform. Of course, particular sectors of capital benefited much more from the process than did others, and some groups grumbled about the new emphasis on export promotion. But all strata of the bourgeoisie welcomed the initial stages of the new development strategy because of its strict depression of wages and its stabilization of the economy.[14] Eventually, losers in the reform process came to include segments of the bourgeoisie who had commanded advantageous niches in the ISI regime and were unable to adapt to the rigors of international competition.[15]

The winners included an upper bourgeoisie – the heart of the so-called 'new right' – that successfully exploited the government's provision of aid and tax breaks to exporting industries. These larger firms also suffered from the contraction of the home market, but were supported by the government and a range of new (post-1980) banks geared to the financing of international trade. These industrialists, in seeking increased government aid and credit, successfully promoted their interests through organizations like TUSIAD (the Turkish Industrialists' and Businessmen's Association).[16]

Though fissures existed in the private sector, TUSIAD succeeded in persuading the various segments of the upper bourgeoisie that the economic reforms would serve their interests. On the whole they controlled the large corporations that were best able to export and compete internationally: for example, the textile industries or Middle Eastern construction firms.[17]

In short, these largest commercial and industrial interests became the driving force behind the economic reforms, and emerged in a dominant position in the post-1983 political system.

The Plight of the Popular Sector

Meanwhile, the state clearly militated against the interests of the popular sector during the early 1980s. In the expansionary 1970s, writes John Waterbury, center-right and center-left coalitions spent public resources 'in a prodigal fashion.' Consequently, between 1974 and 1978, real public sector wages and total employment increased by 58 percent and 28 percent, respectively.[18] In contrast, between 1979 and 1985, wages and employment dropped sharply. Real wages, for example, had declined as a proportion of national income, from 33 percent in 1979 to 18 percent in 1985-6. On one estimate, gross government salaries and wages dropped from 9 percent of GNP in 1979 to 6 percent in 1985. The civil service suffered a 50 percent decline in absolute and relative salaries during these years. The decline in the wages of public sector employees was less dramatic, but substantial none the less. Concomitantly, social welfare provisions were slashed. For example, expenditures on public health and education, as proportions of GDP, declined from 3.3 and 1.1 percent in 1980, to 2.4 and 0.6 percent in 1985. Such expenditures, as Waterbury observes, have been central to the maintenance of social pacts in other times and places.[19]

Unlike bureaucratic-authoritarian regimes in Latin America, the Turkish junta sought a relatively speedy return to civilian government. In relinquishing power, the regime also worked to create a more stable, restrictive and cohesive political system – one that would protect, and indeed complement, the new Turkish economic order. Accordingly, the regime effected sweeping electoral, constitutional and institutional changes.

A restrictive and anti-populist constitution designed by military leaders in 1982 replaced the relatively pro-populist and liberal constitution of 1961.[20] Political restructuring included, *inter alia*, constitutional restrictions on individual liberties; the replacement of a bicameral legislature with a unicameral one; the strengthening of the office of the president; the imposition of tight controls over universities; and far-reaching restrictions on the political, financial, and organizational activities of trade unions and other groups in civil society.

The new political order placed the harshest restrictions on workers and students, the groups that had been most mobilized in the 1970s. The new constitution banned the unions from the political arena: they now were unable to collaborate with any political parties or professional organizations. Further, unions were required to deposit their funds in state-owned banks. Such changes, Barkey observes, 'effectively curbed the unions' bargaining power and helped institutionalize a lesser economic role in society for them, ensuring, in O'Donnell's terms, the economic exclusion of the "popular sectors".'[21]

This new and subservient economic role was based on the diminution of the political power of the popular sectors in the postcoup era. During the transition to civilian rule, the military attempted to redesign the electoral process in ways that empowered the right. To this end, it sponsored the creation of a right-wing party, the Nationalist Democracy Party, which it expected to win the parliamentary elections of 1983.

The goal was a bureaucratic-authoritarian-style political exclusion of the working class. Concerning this new political order, Halit Narin, chairman of the Turkish Employers' Confederation, observed that 'the workers have had their day and now it is our turn.'[22]

In addition to seeking to empower the right, the National Security Council (NSC) also banned politicians of the pre-1980 era from participation in the 1983 elections, and sought the dissolution of the precoup political parties, which were blamed for the political instability and economic mismanagement of the late 1970s. The result was an unprecedented opportunity for those segments of the bourgeoisie who supported the orthodox reforms to capture the state in 1983.

Consolidating the Dominance of the Right

In preparing for the 1983 elections, the military attempted to create a stable two-party system, constituting a center-right party called the Nationalist Democracy Party and a putatively center-left one called the Populist Party. A non-military party, called the Motherland Party (MP) and led by Turgut Ozal, also qualified for the 1983 parliamentary elections. Though the regime strongly preferred the Nationalist Democracy Party, Ozal's party won the election. In winning 45 percent of the popular vote and 211 seats out of a total of 400 in the new parliament, the MP was able to form the first majority government since 1969. The Populist Party won 30 percent of the vote and 117 seats, and the Nationalist Democracy Party received only 24 percent and 71 seats. The Motherland Party, it seems, benefited from the anti-populist electoral codes and practices, and from a public backlash against the military-sponsored parties.[23]

In the end, overlapping factors preserved the coherence of the orthodox restructuring program of the departing military regime in 1983: the enactment of an anti-populist electoral system and constitution; the fact that all three competing parties embraced the regime's stabilization and adjustment programs,[24] and the fact that the only competing party not strongly associated with the military (the MP) was a champion of orthdox reform.

With the reinstatement of parliamentary politics during 1983, the Turkish electoral-constitutional design had become the one most favorable to center-right bourgeois groups in the Middle East. In short, the liberalizing Turkish junta wanted to see the Turkish state remain on a highly orthodox macro-economic path. It therefore designed labor restrictions and electoral laws that blatantly favored right-wing and bourgeoisie-oriented parties. Though the victory of Ozal's Motherland Party came as something of a surprise, the Turkish generals did accomplish their objective of empowering center-right bourgeois groups and orthodoxy-oriented policy-makers. And in an era of ISI decline in the Middle East (and throughout the Third World), such an outcome should be considered a hallmark of electoral openings in a minimally rentier system.

MOROCCO: POLITICAL LIBERALIZATION IN A MINIMALLY RENTIER STATE

If and when the levels of exogenous rents decline in the region's semi-rentier states, those countries should move toward either the democratic model represented by minimally rentier Turkey or toward the authoritarian model represented by the minimally rentier Morocco. Morocco is particularly relevant to contemporary cases of Middle Eastern political change in its demonstration of how electoral authoritarianism can be used to legitimate increasingly austere center-right development policies. That is, the Moroccan case dramatizes the confluence of central regional trends, those of economic neoliberalism, anti-populism, and limited political liberalization.

The pivotal political-economic events of 1983-4 should be considered within the context of the regime's traditional approaches to development and the popular sectors. By regional standards, the regime had during the 1960s and 1970s been particularly negligent in its welfare provisions, especially in the fields of health, housing, and education.[25] The 1970s saw a tremendous expansion of the Moroccan public sector, financed above all by domestic and international creditors. But unlike Arab states such as Egypt, Morocco never developed an elaborate 'social contract' that improved and protected the prospects of the popular sectors.[26] Consequently, the austerity imposed in 1983-84 had initiated an especially right-wing political-economic order in Morocco.

Economic crisis in fact began to trouble the government as early as 1976. Rapid economic growth in the mid-1970s, spurred by public spending and financed by external borrowings, was followed by a sharp drop in export earnings from phosphates and agricultural products during 1976-7.[27] In 1978, the state faced a severe resource gap (roughly 20 percent of GDP) and began to cut public expenditures in most sectors, except on a continued military buildup. Economic growth then decelerated rapidly.[28] By the early 1980s, the Moroccan economic crisis had been augmented by external factors, including a severe drought, the escalation of the Saharan war, declining phosphate earnings, rising oil-import costs, and a global recession. Meanwhile, the external debt had grown precipitously, increasing from $1.2 billion in 1981 to $9 billion by 1983, and to $13 billion in 1984. During 1983-4, external loans covered most of the treasury and balance-of-payments deficits, and the debt-service ratio reached roughly 47 percent. By 1983, foreign exchange levels had reached their lowest levels since independence. The government was forced by 1984 to borrow annually about $3 billion simply to service its debt.[29]

Finally, amid the economic troubles of the early 1980s, the Moroccan state was particularly susceptible to vagaries in Saudi foreign aid, which had become its most important source of exogenous revenues. Morocco typically received more than $500 miliion annually in Saudi foreign aid during the late 1970s.[30] But Saudi Arabia dramatically increased its provisions in 1980 and 1981, in response to the escalation of the war in the Western Sahara. Morocco thus received $894 million in foreign aid (including some small official loans) from all sources in 1980, and just over $1 billion in 1981. But in 1982, Saudi Arabia slashed its aid. By 1983-4, Morocco was receiving less than $400 million per annum in total aid, though a free six-month supply of Saudi oil offset this loss to an extent in 1984.[31]

Of course, the decline in aid was not the cause of the Moroccan economic crisis, which began in the late 1970s. As indicated above, structural problems in the Moroccan economy, a global recession, and several years of drought and poor harvest were the central factors. But the drop in Saudi giving, coupled with the spending of about 40 percent of the annual budget on the Saharan campaign, did augment the crisis.

Toward Moroccan Orthodoxy

Facing an insurmountable resource gap, the state had no choice but to reschedule its debt and enter into a series of negotiations with its official and private creditors, beginning in 1983. As Ahmed Rhazaoui observes, the result was Moroccan acceptance of an orthodox development package that much resembled the tough neoclassical prescriptions imposed on other heavily indebted Third World countries.[32] The goals of the agreements included the development of an export-oriented strategy; the almost total opening of the economy to the international market through the reduction of tariff and nontariff barriers; the encouragement of the private sector; and the substantial reduction of consumption and government spending.

In other words, the economic reforms of the early 1980s were diverse and in many respects sweeping. For example, the July 1983 budget cut public expenditures by 12.5 percent, to Dh46.1 billion; and the 1984 budget further reduced expenditures to Dh43.8 billion.[33] In 1983, the government froze wages and hiring, and eliminated 8600 government posts. Moroccan officials claim that austerity measures increased unemployment by 2 percent, but observers believe that the increase was considerably higher. The unemployment rate was estimated at 29.6 percent in 1984, and as high as 40 percent in 1987.[34] Spending on health and housing declined in real terms and in relation to total expenditures (though education investments rose, reflecting significant enrollment increases).[35] The dirham was devalued, customs duties and other import restrictions were reduced, and investment codes were revised in order to encourage foreign investment. As well, the government sought to stimulate the 'productive' (private) sector, easing the tax burden on exporting firms and cancelling taxes on agricultural businesses.[36]

Economists continue to debate whether the Moroccan structural changes will be in the long-term interests of the population at large. Clearly, however, the readjustment and stabilization policies had the immediate effect of imposing a harsh austerity on the popular sectors, and of catering to the most powerful segments of Moroccan society.[37] Here the strident austerity of Moroccan neoliberalism has resembled the anti-populist nature of economic reforms in minimally rentier Turkey, and has consistently been more far-reaching and anti-populist than that of semi-rentier Egypt. For as I argue in the section below on Egypt, the Mubarak regime has been able to use exogenous rents to maintain a relatively 'pro-populist' stance.

The bread riots of January 1984, like the riots of 1981, did slow the regime's push toward neoliberal orthodoxy. Most importantly, despite IMF pressure, the regime did not eliminate basic food subsidies for fear of popular protest. In the end, Morocco's Western allies and creditors clearly sought to prevent the destabilization of King Hassan's regime. Still, the economic crisis was such that, in the words of an OECD report, austerity, stabilization, and restructuring had become 'unavoidable.'[38] At the same time, King Hassan faced the task of creating a political order that legitimated the neoliberal economic program. Parliamentary elections were scheduled for 1981, but were postponed for two years as rising social tensions had put the regime in an increasingly untenable position. After elections were again postponed in 1983, 12 political parties contested what was, by Moroccan standards, a relatively open and vigorous campaign and polling in 1984. At the same time, the regime succeeded in creating parliamentary support for its new development programs, by manufacturing the vote, gerrymandering single-member constituencies, manipulating the campaign process, and forming a new dominant party.

Indeed, the crown's subtle yet masterly conduct of the September polling worked to defuse much of the political tension in the kingdom. The riots of the early 1980s had targeted the regime's austere or negligent economic and social policies. Yet the 1984 polling succeeded in legitimating a defense of those policies, and political instability abated during the following years.

The Constitutional Union and the New Right

The cornerstone of this effort was the Constitutional Union (UC), which prime minister Maati Bouabid created in 1983 at the direction of the royal palace. Alain Claisse notes that 'a circular from the prime minister invited heads of departments, general secretaries, and their fellow workers to join the new party.'[39] The Constitutional Union sought to incorporate and unify key factions of an urban elite that would be supportive of the 1983 austerity package and of the new economic directions in general. At the same time, the prime minister attempted to create an 'independent' network of party 'cadres' among Morocco's professional stratum.[40] Ideologically, the Constitutional Union embraced both political and economic liberalizations, as these 'complementary' processes were deemed essential to the consolidation of Moroccan 'democracy.'[41]

That Mohammed Karim Lamrani promptly replaced Bouabid as prime minister following the founding of the party was not surprising. A central feature of Moroccan politics was, and is, the king's traditional and constitutional position above and beyond the party system. By extension, writes Rkia El-Mossadeq, the prime minister has been nonpartisan, 'a faithful servant of the king.'[42] Bouabid's replacement reflected a traditional desire of the king 'not to be identified directly with any of the new parties created by a prime minister while in office.'[43] Clearly, it did not suggest the crown's disavowal of the Constitutional Union as the centerpiece of the new loyalist alignment. Accordingly, throughout the 1980s the new 'nonpartisan' prime minister championed the reformist programs of the Constitutional Union.

Ultimately, the crown's provision of support, patronage, and legitimacy was instrumental in the UC's triumph among a traditionally fragmented electorate in 1984. Despite its newness and lack of popular support, the party received 27 percent of both the popular and 'indirect' balloting. (To ensure acceptable electoral results, as I discuss below, one-third of parliamentary seats are chosen indirectly by local councils and assemblies.) The UC thus won 83 of the 306 parliamentary seats.

The Rassemblement National des Independants (RNI) was the second biggest winner in 1984, obtaining 61 seats. Dominated by long-time associates of the king and men from some of Morocco's wealthiest families, the RNI has pledged 'unconditional loyalty' to King Hassan. As Mark Tessler observes, the RNI is 'more of an electoral front than an institutionalized political party.' It was organized to mobilize a majority from the 140 'king's men' elected in 1977 to the 264-member parliament, and was led by prime minister Ahmad Osman, the king's confidante and brother-in-law. Intended to represent the post-independence generation of the 'New Morocco,' the RNI foreshadowed the regime's reorganization of the loyalist right through the Constitutional Union in 1983.[44] But having splintered in 1981, the RNI never developed into anything more than a parliamentary club. The regime accordingly shifted its electoral efforts to the UC in 1984.

The other parties that joined the governing coalition in 1984 were the Parti National Democratique (PND), which won 24 seats, and the Mouvement Populaire (MP), which won 47 seats. The PND was dominated by rural royalist elites who broke away from the RNI in 1981. Similarly, conservative elites dominated the so-called Berberist MP, which protected the interest of a rural pro-government bourgeoisie. (The MP has had a more institutionalized electoral base, especially among Berbers, than have the RNI and the PND.) Most of the dominant players of the RNI, the PND, and MP hailed from Morocco's leading capitalist families, and have been incorporated within the crown's patronage network.[45]

The UC became the organizational and ideological center of this royalist coalition. Its success was largely at the expense of the royalist parties like the

RNI and the PND, whose central ideology is loyalty to the crown. Younger and better organized than those of the other parties, the cadres of the UC sought to make a grassroots appeal for economic and social reform during the 1984 campaign. It was intended to compete in the cities against the established opposition parties, the Istiqlal and the USFP (described below). Preparations for the UC's 1983 inauguration reportedly had been underway since 1980. On one estimate, roughly 10000 professionals, advanced civil servants, teachers, and private sector managers – approximately one-fifth of these sectors – attended the founding event.[46]

In the end, though more institutionalized than the RNI and PND, the Constitutional Union's attempt to penetrate and incorporate an extensive network of social groups met with mixed success. It did constitute an effective reorganization of the political elite, but remained at the same time dependent on royal patronage. Its neoliberal program supported the regime's push to reform the economy, and by and large served the interests of the various coalition constituents. The coalition was, in turn, the streamlined center-right political order that the regime had forged in order to weather the development crisis of the 1980s. Though never evolving into a dynamic popular movement, it did oversee and legitimate a positively crucial policy shift, from the relatively populist and expansionary model of the 1970s to the austere and neoliberal one of the 1980s and 1990s. In this sense, the creation of the UC was a critical success.

The Opposition

The opposition was composed of the two parties that are most institutionalized and are least dependent on the crown's patronage. As I. William Zartman argues, both the Istiqlal and the Socialist Union of Popular Forces (USFP) are more institutionalized than the royalist parties, in the sense that popular participation and mobilization are a larger part of their daily activities. Each party has 'ongoing constituency relations and functioning cells' that support the party hierarchy and their elected representatives.[47] The regime's bias toward the right in 1984, I argue below, was readily apparent in its treatment of the two parties of the opposition, as it was in its shaping of the royalist coalition.

The Istiqlal party, having grown out of the anti-colonial struggle against France, represented a center-right opposition to the crown, but had not, by and large, opposed the regime's neoliberal reforms in the early 1980s. The Istiqlal had done reasonably well in the 1977 elections – winning 49 seats and becoming the second largest party – primarily because of its strong stand on the Saharan issue. But the party lost popularity in the early 1980s, largely because of its conservative ideology in the years of economic austerity.

Furthermore, the Istiqlal's credibility among the electorate had been sapped by its participation in the government from 1976 until 1983.[48] Still, in winning 41 seats in 1984, the Istiqlal was the fourth largest party in parliament. A reasonable speculation is that the regime ensured the mild success of this 'waning'[49] party in 1984, largely because the Istiqlal maintained a compatible stance on the pressing issues of economic reform. In the indirect elections in particular, as I discuss below, the regime predictably favored the Istiqlal over the USFP, the sole parliamentary force supporting relatively populist policies.

On the left of the political spectrum, the USFP was widely considered the most important and genuinely popular political party in Morocco.[50] It represented 'a boundary marker for the system,'[51] writes Zartman, in its being the most oppositional of the major legitimate political forces in Morocco. After winning but 16 seats in the 1977 elections, the USFP obtained 36 seats in 1984, becoming the fifth largest party in the parliament. Zartman argues that the dramatic increase in the representation of the USFP signalled the king's desire to reach out to the 'marginal, cynical, or even alienated'[52] masses who were cut off from the dominant parties of the king's men. In an attempt to legitimate the new government, King Hassan even sought the USFP's participation in the majority coalition, an eventuality precluded by the USFP's opposition to the regime's neoliberalism. Accordingly, after the elections, the party bitterly attacked the government's overall development strategy. In early 1985, the USFP's 38 representatives were the only members of the new parliament who voted against the new readjustment package.[53]

Symbolism and polemics notwithstanding, the center-right parties thoroughly dominated the USFP's small representation. Its status in the parliament improved again following the 1993 elections. But in the most critical years of economic crisis and austerity, the USFP as the representative of the populist center-left seemed neatly and inevitably relegated to a peripheral parliamentary status.

In the end, the minimally rentier Moroccan regime, like the Turkish one, had given an ascendant electoral position to center-right bourgeois groups espousing neoliberal reforms. That is, they were best able to exercise the rights of political expression and participation offered by the political openings in the region's minimally rentier states. Here the Turkish and Moroccan regimes sought an orthodox coalition: engineering a right-wing dominance of parliament and relying on financial supports from international creditors. In addition, each minimally rentier regime sought to reorganize and rationalize interest representation on the center-right. The goal was the creation of an alliance against the popular sectors, one that would comply with the demands of international capital.

EGYPT: ELECTORAL POLITICS IN A SEMI-RENTIER POLITY

The regime of President Hosni Mubarak was a tightrope walk of sorts in the 1980s. Economic inefficiency pushed Egypt, like countries throughout the Third World, to develop increasingly intimate ties with the international creditor community. Meanwhile, exogenous rents, derived primarily from an oil industry, the country's geopolitical situation, and the Suez Canal, enabled the regime to dilute and postpone the political-economic measures demanded by that community, and adopted more vigorously by the region's minimally rentier states. Here Egypt used exogenous resources to maintain much of its 'social contract' and welfare state, even as its economy has become increasingly controlled by the international financial community. In sum, unlike the Moroccan and Turkish regimes, the Mubarak regime attempted to cling to a 'populist' political position.

My consideration of Egypt as a semi-rentier electoral system focuses primarily on the 1984 resumption of parliamentary politics under Mubarak. The 1984 contest marked the reopening of the Egyptian political system, in the sense that it fully reversed the serious setbacks to the political liberalization process that began to occur in 1979, and culminated in the severe crackdown on opposition groups and the assassination of President Anwar Sadat in 1981.

Mubarak revived and consolidated, but did not alter, the basic structure of Sadat's controlled multiparty electoral system. He sought, as Daniel Brumberg puts it, 'a more consistent policy of "democratic accommodation"' with bourgeois opposition forces.[54] This diverse and fragmented stratum, moreover, has emerged as the most politically articulate sector of Egyptian society,[55] and one whose resources are important to the regime's development program. At the same time, the regime has adopted different strategies in its dealings with specific segments of this class. In particular, a center-right bourgeoisie, composed of groups seeking the implementation of orthodox macroeconomic policies, has become the focal point for parliamentary opposition to the regime and its development policies.

In brief, through the 1984 elections, the regime gave these center-right groups a privileged but *oppositional* role within the parliament. As I. William Zartman observes, an alternative parliamentary strategy would have embraced a right-wing ideology, and sought the cooptation of the leadership of pro-orthodox forces. Instead, he argues, the 1984 elections enabled the regime to 'defend itself against the right as a center-left party.' It was, to his mind, 'an example of the ultimate use of the opposition to define the government.'[56]

Here exogenous revenues enabled the Egyptian regime to avoid the adoption of a center-right parliamentary strategy, and to postpone and mitigate the disruptive process of economic restructuring.

In the Turkish and Moroccan cases, a relative lack of exogenous rents placed greater fiscal pressures on the regimes, which then perforce sought more intensive relations with the international creditor community. In turn, these two regimes were forced to legitimate relatively unpopular orthodox development strategies within their electoral openings. The Moroccan and Turkish regimes compensated for their unpopular development agendas by maintaining powerful authoritarian controls over the electoral process, and by using alternative ideological appeals (for example, against the 'disruptive' Turkish left or to the religious legitimacy of the Moroccan crown).

By contrast, while using similar authoritarian controls, the Egyptian regime was able to avoid the adoption within the parliament of a risky and unpopular development agenda, one that had been associated, for example, with the 1977 food riots. Of course, the victory of the regime's National Democratic Party (NDP) was never in doubt. Rather, the interesting aspect of the 1984 election was the regime's creation of a center-right opposition, one that enabled the regime to portray itself as being a center-left protector of the popular sector.

The Rentier Windfalls of the Early 1980s

A relatively propitious economy in the few years preceding the 1984 elections enabled the regime to adopt this strategy. While Morocco and Turkey were in the throes of economic crisis, Egypt was experiencing rapid growth: about 8 percent a year during the late 1970s and early 1980s. The country was 'leaving other developing countries in the dust,'[57] one observer noted. But its growth, he added, was being driven by exogenous resources, most importantly, oil revenues and US aid. Indeed, state access to exogenous resources had reached unprecedented levels by the early 1980s – and in turn declined during the middle 1980s.[58] Following Sadat's assassination, the Mubarak regime relied on this windfall to consolidate its control. While Turkey and Morocco were imposing austerity, Egypt increased popular consumption and the provision of social services. Food subsidies, for example, had begun to claim more than 15 percent of total government expenditures: E L1.5 billion in 1983 and E L1.7 billion in 1984. The bread subsidy in itself outstripped Suez Canal rents. 'Dirt-cheap' energy was thought to account for another E L2 billion in 'hidden' subsidies. Consumer spending rose to 70 percent of GDP during the early 1980s.[59]

Despite the strong economic growth, increased consumption created financial difficulties for the government in 1984. Since merchandise imports rose precipitously and merchandise exports increased only moderately, the government faced growing balance-of-payment and trade-deficit problems. It was, for example, unable to pay suppliers' credits or service its US military debt.[60] Consequently, in 1984, the IMF attempted to persuade government to implement mild economic reforms which would curb consumption and improve the balance-of-payment situation.

More broadly, of course, the Egyptian economy faced long-term structural difficulties that were comparable to, if not greater than, those confronting the Moroccan and Turkish economies. A vast state sector, and an ISI model incapable of generating sufficient foreign exchange, produced enduring inefficiency. But Egypt's exogenous revenues simply cushioned the shocks of global recession during the early 1980s.[61]

Unlike the ambitious Turkish and Moroccan restructuring of the early and mid-1980s, Egypt's reforms were extremely limited and at times purely cosmetic. The IMF, for example, persuaded the government to devalue the pound to spur exports and curb consumption. Meanwhile, in defying IMF demands for a single free-market rate, Egypt made its system of multiple exchange rates even more complicated. The most controversy centered around the issue of food subsidies. A 1984 report of the International Food Policy Research Institute argued that these rising subsidies had created a powerful impediment to economic growth, by sucking in food imports, increasing the budget deficit, and harming local industry and public financing.

At the behest of the IMF, the government announced cuts in subsidies in September of 1984. In response, several thousand people participated in riots on September 29–30 in a Nile Delta town. Though these demonstrations were less significant than the 1977 Cairo riots, Mubarak did cancel the cuts in subsidies. The regime promptly promised that food prices would remain stable, and that indeed the cost of butter and pasta would be reduced. In another gesture to the popular sectors, the regime slapped higher taxes on the upper classes.[62]

In sum, the economic imbalances created by increases in consumption during the late 1970s and early 1980s, did not force Egypt to develop an anti-populist program. The Mubarak regime used the windfalls of the early 1980s to consolidate its position, and indeed succeeded in postponing almost all far-reaching reforms until the early 1990s.

Manufacturing a 'Populist' Parliamentary Majority and an Orthodox Opposition

A careful manufacturing of the 1984 elections gave the opposition about 27 percent of the valid votes and 13 percent of the elected seats in the People's Assembly. The regime permitted four opposition parties – the New Wafd, Liberal, Socialist Labor, and Nationalist Progressive Unionist Parties – to contest the elections. Since the regime set an 8 percent threshold for the obtaining of seats, only the center-right New Wafd, with 15.12 percent of the vote, was able to win representation in the Assembly. A representative of various center-right bourgeois interests, this party became the sole significant oppositional voice.

The 1984 economic program of the New Wafd strongly resembled those of its center-right counterparts in Morocco and Turkey. It championed capitalist free-market reforms and attacked the predominant statist legacies from the Nasirist era. As a firm backer of the *Infitah* policies, it advocated, among other things, cuts in government subsidies, the adoption of an export-led strategy, and the curbing of government intervention in the economy. Against these calls, the dominant NDP mounted a putatively 'populist' defense, one that resisted the onslaught of a reactionary national bourgeoisie and the unyielding demands of international forces.[63]

Giving the NDP's posturing against the right some power was the fact that the parties of the left – or at any rate, the parties left of the NDP – were unable to win a single parliamentary seat. The regime's manueverings in the spring of 1984, and its redesign of the electoral laws in 1983, effectively eliminated a leftist alternative to the NDP in the May elections. The most important changes were the new 8 percent threshold and the replacement of 175 electoral districts with a proportional representation system in which voters choose party lists. Having previously concentrated their campaign efforts in those districts they were likely to win, the leftist National Progressive Unionist Party and the center-left Socialist Labor Party were now forced to compete across all electoral districts.[64] These parties were simply too weak to compete successfully in such a national system, and their leaderships well understood the regime's purposive exclusion of their voices from the parliament.[65] Having led the pre-independence nationalist movement, the New Wafd commanded more resources than the other opposition parties, and was better able to cope with the regime's controls over the electoral process. (Thus, during the campaign, most of the support for the right-wing Liberal Party defected to the New Wafd.) Finally, the regime's electoral machine ensured that the final electoral results would exclude the leftists.[66]

The 'Center-left' versus the Right

After the 1984 elections the New Wafd claimed that it had become the 'national alternative' to the NDP. Or rather, as one party newspaper editorial put it, the resurgent party was prepared to win the coming parliamentary elections and to reassume its rightful dominance of Egyptian politics.[67] At the same time, the Mubarak regime did not permit a coherent pro-orthodox center-right to participate in, much less create, the new government; for much of the regime's leadership in fact opposed far-reaching economic liberalization. Rather, the regime made the New Wafd a 'corrective' and 'complementary'[68] opposition.

Thus, the Egyptian regime's parliamentary and developmental strategies were more 'populist' or center-left than those of the two minimally rentier states. At the same time, solely in the context of Egyptian political development, the Mubarak regime has been relatively conservative and center-right. That is, it has slowly and fitfully moved away from its Nasirist and Arab socialist roots. But from my perspective, that movement would have been more rapid and dynamic, if the regime had had access to lower levels of exogenous rents.

KUWAIT: ELECTORAL POLITICS IN A HIGHLY RENTIER POLITY

The third category under consideration, which I am calling 'highly rentier,' refers to those Middle Eastern states receiving the vast majority of their revenues from exogenous rents. These states of the Persian/Arabian Gulf typically receive over 70 percent, and sometimes over 95 percent, of their total revenues from nonproductive sources, particularly petroleum reserves and overseas investments. In considering the link between economic resources and controlled electoral politics in such states, this section discusses the ability of the Kuwaiti regime to use an electoral system to undermine the political power of a well-established Kuwaiti business and merchant elite. It first notes key historical developments in the representational politics of Kuwait, and then considers the reinstatement of the Kuwaiti National Assembly in 1981 and the regime's suspension of the body in 1986.

I consider Kuwait's electoral experiments to be indicative of how the other Arabian monarchies might design limited political openings in the distant future. Such openings are able to assume forms that do not exist in the other countries in the region. They may well principally reflect tribal and sectarian alliances, and attempt to marginalize threatening class actors such as an emergent bourgeoisie. (In Chapter 6, I show how the parliament of post-revolution Iran fits this pattern.) A highly rentier state is able to exercise these options, because of its seemingly unlimited exogenous resources.

The Political Power of the Kuwaiti Bourgeoisie

A legislative assembly first emerged in Kuwait during the 1930s, largely because of the mobilization of important merchant and business families seeking to check the power of the ruling Al Sabah family. Historically, the central power behind these families has been a group of eight families, known as the *aseel* or the 'original': Al Saqer, Al Khalid, Al Nisif, Al Ghanim, Al Hamad, Al Mudhaf, Al Khorafi, and Al Marzouk.[69] Originally from the Najd region of Saudi Arabia, these families have considered themselves to be the founders of Kuwait, and have sought to maintain their privileged political and economic status in Kuwaiti society. Parallel networks of merchant families are of different ethnic origin, but trace their roots to the early days of the principality, and have occupied comparable economic and social positions. Together, they and the *aseel* represent an old, urban, Sunni elite that traditionally included merchants, sea traders, and landowners.[70] These families, known as the Bani Utub, distinguished themselves from 'newcomers' who flocked to Kuwait because of its oil wealth. Additional social and confessional factors separated this economic elite from other Kuwaiti groups: they were Sunni and not Shia; and urban and sedentary, and not nomadic or Beduin. Through shared economic interests and intermarriage, the Bani Utub became a homogenized and unified force in a relatively diverse society.[71]

The Bani Utub and Al Sabah family were the traditional political powers of the pre-oil era. According to one tradition, the establishment of Kuwait as a political entity occurred in 1756, when the Bani Utub chose a Sabah as the shaikh of the principality.[72] In general, before the emergence of the contemporary oil-rich society, Al Sabah rule depended on the consent and cooperation of the merchant community. The financial power of the merchants, in particular, limited the pre-eminence of the Al Sabah rulers. Their influence, notes Jill Crystal, 'came from their control of trade and imports, duties on which sustained the Shaik.'[73] Dependence on the taxation of the merchant and business community, in other words, was the historical basis for checks on the power of Kuwaiti rulers. Before the arrival of oil wealth, she argues, 'the struggle between the rulers and the emerging bourgeoisie was following a classic pattern,'[74] as the merchants used their economic resources to obtain political power.

The Oil Revolution and the Political Decline of the Bourgeoisie

Oil wealth, however, transformed Kuwaiti power relations during the mid-twentieth century. It flowed directly to the Al Sabah family and augmented its power in relation to all Kuwaiti social groups. But the royal family, in particular, has used contemporary parliamentary politics to dilute and marginalize the political power of the Bani Utub. Once the pre-eminent rival and partner of the royal family, the business/merchant class has become one of several groups of 'commoners' assuming 'oppositional' parliamentary roles.

Crystal has identified the origins of Kuwaiti parliamentary politics in the pre-independence *Majlis* Movement, which prominent Bani Utub merchants formed in 1938 in order to demand a say in the distribution of the new oil revenues. The Movement created a short-lived legislative Assembly, which succeeded in introducing a number of reforms that improved the economic, social, and educational conditions of the merchant community. Though Shaikh Ahmad dissolved the Assembly on December 17, 1938, the Movement created powerful coalitional and institutional legacies. Most importantly, as Crystal observes, the merchant families realized that they could 'formalize' and 'institutionalize' their access to the regime. The result was a 'streamlined and homogenized' merchant community that emerged as the 'most coherent and organized political force in Kuwaiti society.'[75]

As a result, the merchant elite maintained powerful ties to the rulers. They had demonstrated that they were 'the one group capable of sustained, organized, and possibly successful opposition.'[76] Following Kuwaiti independence in June of 1961, the ruling family sought to weaken its position through the creation of a commoners' National Assembly. The Al Sabah expected the Assembly to legitimate, and set the boundaries of, the political system in several ways: for example, to satisfy a demand for political expression and participation, especially among the Bani Utub; to distinguish between the minority of Kuwaiti citizens and the majority of expatriate laborers (who do not have political rights); and to distinguish between commoners and the Al Sabah, who have never served in the body.

Crystal observes that the regime forged a tacit agreement with the merchant families, providing them with largesse in exchange for their marginalization in political life: 'the merchants were bought off, by the state, as a class.'[77] Throughout most of the 1950s and 1960s, the state purchased the lands of the merchant community at tremendously inflated prices. Such purchases indeed constituted the largest state expenditure during these years. The private sector 'became the playground for the merchants.'[78] In return, notes Crystal, the royal family demanded the withdrawal of the merchants from political life. The regime used oil revenues to buy political autonomy from the merchants, observes Mary Ann Tetreault, in the same way that it has attempted to use such largesse to buy or preserve its autonomy in the international arena.[79]

The merchants maintained a strong sense of community, even as oil wealth began to transform Kuwait. In effect, state largesse helped the Bani Utub to become a business class, one that has dominated modern Kuwaiti trade and finance. The Al Sabah family apparently agreed to refrain from encroaching on the community's singular control over the private sector, and to ensure its privileged access to government contracts. This informal agreement between the regime and the merchants worked to consolidate the Bani Utub's control over the domestic economy, but was, it seems, violated by members of the royal family in the late 1970s and 1980s.

As Tetreault notes, Jabir Ahmad, whose rule began in 1977, tolerated the royal family's increased penetration into the private sector. The regime's violation of the informal agreement in turn increased tensions between it and much of the Bani Utub members in the 1980s.[80]

Conversely, the regime used formal political life to enhance the political status of groups that had occupied disadvantaged political and socioeconomic positions during the pre-oil era. This process originated in the creation of the Kuwaiti parliament in 1961 and continued to dominate the political openings of the 1970s and 1980s. A key function of the first Assembly, observes Crystal, 'was to draw a distinction between the merchants and other politically important groups and to serve as a vehicle for balancing and, in part, replacing them with new, more controllable allies.'[81] This function in fact was reaffirmed in subsequent Assemblies, as the ruling family bequeathed assembly seats to different groups, be they Beduins, Shias, religious conservatives, progessive nationalists and so forth.

Crystal notes that the advent of Kuwaiti parliamentary politics in 1963 initiated a process of 'retribalization' in which disadvantaged tribes 'were able to trade electoral support for massive housing, social services, scholarships, and jobs, especially as soldiers, police officers, guards, and bodyguards.'[82] In other words, the Al Sabah family has been able to use state resources to orient Kuwaiti electoral politics around tribal and sectarian issues and to de-emphasize socioeconomic inequalities. Exogenous rents have, by and large, enabled the regime to pacify the material demands of Kuwaiti social groups. State patronage, furthermore, has procured the loyalty of the traditionally disadvantaged sectors.

These attributes are classic features of the rentier state as described in the original literature on the subject. The rise of oil wealth effectively stymied movement toward a parliament dominated by the economic elite. Like its rough counterparts in some Western countries and in Britain in particular, the Kuwaiti bourgeoisie had led, indeed embodied, the pre-oil struggle for a form of representative government. Not only has the ruling family's control over the country's oil wealth retribalized Kuwaiti politics and consolidated the security of the authoritarian regime, through an extensive patronage system, it has also enabled the regime to develop methods for the evisceration of the merchant elite as the political power that had once challenged the ruling family.

The 1981 Elections: Consolidating Beduin Dominance of Parliament

Though 447 candidates competed for 50 Assembly seats, the regime carefully controlled the 1981 opening. Observers debate whether the electoral process had been 'clean' or 'fair.' But it did, without a doubt, use various mechanisms, especially the gerrymandering of 25 electoral districts, to promote conservative and anti-Shia tribal and sectarian allies.[83]

An increase in the overrepresentation of Beduins, who won 28 seats, was the principal electoral outcome. As a relatively small Kuwaiti minority, they had controlled, on one estimate, roughly 50 percent of the seats in the four previous parliaments.[84] Though this overrepresentation had fueled a Beduin-urban rivalry in the previous Assembly, the regime abetted the increase of Beduin members to 56 percent through the creation of additional electoral districts in rural areas.[85]

The 1981 Assembly also included six Sunni Islamists, three Arab nationalists, and two Shias. Shias were the biggest losers in 1981. Having controlled roughly 20 percent of the seats during the previous four Assemblies, they won merely 8 percent of the seats in 1981. At the same time, Beduins and Sunni Islamists accounted for more than two-thirds of the Assembly members. The 1981 Assembly was, in other words, an attempt to manufacture a cultural-sectarian identity that would support a regime buffeted by the Iranian revolution.[86] It is also important to note that the regime has used the electoral process to reaffirm the distinction between citizens and non-citizens. For example only 90 000 men of a total population of 1.35 million were eligible to vote in 1981.[87]

Young 'technocrats,' including two representatives of the merchant elite, won 13 seats.[88] Despite their presence, the issues of economic development and business interests were of minor importance to the Kuwaiti electoral process of the 1980s. Central concerns included tribal rivalries, security, corruption, Islamism, and the conduct of foreign affairs. Further, the merchant representatives found that the Assembly was an unfavorable venue for the defense of their economic interests.[89]

Interpreting Class and Ideology in Kuwait

Interpreting the right and left, or the upper and popular classes is somewhat complicated in the Kuwaiti case. Tribal Beduin groups dominated Kuwait's parliament and enjoyed the regime's patronage in the 1980s. Compared to noncitizens, who are the majority of the Kuwaiti population, Beduins are hardly disadvantaged, politically, economically, or otherwise. In relation to other citizens, however, they have been – and remain – greatly disadvantaged in terms of employment, income, education, social status, and so forth. Thus, within the Kuwaiti oligarchy, the Beduin occupy the lowest social stratum.[90]

As such, they are often quite hostile toward the highly cohesive bourgeoisie.[91] Overlapping class and ethnic identities divide the urban Sunni merchants and the tribal Beduins, who disagree over such basic policy questions as the provision of welfare.[92] Further, the regime enfranchised many Beduin groups to marginalize and isolate the bourgeoisie in the political system.

In the end, and unlike the electoral experiments in the semi- and minimally rentier states, the Kuwaiti opening of 1981 was not designed to offer bourgeois groups a powerful and distinctive role in parliamentary politics. Though they had represented the most important political power after the royal family during the pre-oil era, they were now one of several rivals in the Assembly and in political life in general.

Appropriately, the Kuwaiti regime dramatically increased the kinds of populist expenditures that Turkish and Moroccan regimes decreased and that the Egyptian regime indulged cautiously. Before the 1981 elections, the regime proposed dramatic increases in basic local subsidies in an attempt to solidify its support among tribal allies. Subsequently, despite declining revenues, state expenditures increased by 30 percent, as the new parliament endorsed highly expansionary budgets.[93] The minimally rentier states, by contrast, slashed such consumer provisions in the months preceding their political openings; and the Egyptian state, wary of the response of its creditors, made guarded concessions to popular groups in preparing for the 1984 opening.

1985-6: Parliamentary Collapse

The 1981-5 Assembly was relatively tame and cooperative. The political opening succeeded in manufacturing the tribal and sectarian support the regime had sought in order to weather the regional upheaval of the early 1980s. In the 1985 Assembly elections, however, forces hostile to the regime advanced. Sunni and Shia Islamists increased their representation slightly and became increasingly hostile toward the government. Secular nationalist, liberal, and leftist forces (as represented, for example, by the pro-democracy Graduates Society) also made significant gains. Two prominent merchant representatives remained;[94] and the size of the Beduin bloc, in obtaining roughly 27 seats,[95] stayed fairly constant as well. Still, the overall result was an increasingly critical and strident Assembly.

Members representing the major Kuwaiti business and merchant groups soon joined Islamists and nationalists in attacking the regime, as they resented the encroachment of segments of the ruling family into the business sector. The regime's Beduin supporters also became increasingly critical. Consequently, in July of 1986, the regime dissolved the troublesome institution that had been designed to provide it with tribal and sectarian support. The business and merchant elite promptly signalled its approval of the demise of a parliament that had never really represented them, by staging a rally on the Kuwaiti stock market.[96]

In the end, the regime has used the National Assembly, over the decades, to strengthen its alliances against the elite Bani Utub families, and to weaken the political power of the merchant and business class. The advent of the National

Assembly in 1963 ultimately worked to effect the decline of the merchants' political fortunes. That decline has been all the more striking, given the fact that the merchant and business class had been, after the royal family, the pre-eminent political power and had embodied the parliamentary movement during the pre-oil era. By the 1980s, this class had been reduced to one of several Kuwaiti 'oppositional' forces. In contrast, the semi-rentier and minimally rentier political openings tend, as I have argued, to give important electoral-political roles to bourgeois groups, and to enhance their political fortunes.

Unlike semi- or minimally rentier states, a highly rentier one is not forced to offer electoral concessions to bourgeois groups to secure their participation in, or cooperation with, the state's development plan. Further, the highly rentier state has a unique ability to indulge in populist policies. In the event, as state revenues declined in the early 1980s, state expenditure increased quite substantially.

CONCLUSION

The post-ISI global economy has forced developing countries to pursue increasingly orthodox development strategies. This chapter has demonstrated how external capital flows have enabled some developing countries to resist the prevailing reformist trends. In turn, exogenous revenues have been instrumental in creating distinctive development patterns in the Middle East. Rent-poor regimes have been more likely to move toward the global economic orthodoxy and toward orthodox-oriented parliamentary forms. Relatively rent-rich regimes have been better able to avoid orthodox market reforms and to maintain populist political coalitions.

NOTES

1. For example, compare the contrasting views of Muharrem Tunay in 'The New Turkish Right's Attempt at Hegemony,' in Atila Erlap, Muharrem Tunay, and Birol Yesilada (eds), *The Political and Economic Transformation of Turkey*, Westport, CT: Praeger, 1993; and Andrew Mango, 'The Social Democratic Populist Party, 1983–1989,' in Metin Heper and Jacob Landau (eds), *Political Parties and Democracy in Turkey*, London: I.B. Tauris, 1991.
2. For a detailed analysis, see Henri J. Barkey, *The State and the Industrialization Crisis in Turkey*, New York: St. Martin's Press, 1992, pp. 79–104.
3. Ziya Onis, 'Redemocratization and Economic Liberalization in Turkey: the Limits of State Autonomy,' *Studies in Comparative International Development*, 27(2) (Summer 1992), 8.
4. See Henri J. Barkey, 'State Autonomy and the Crisis of Import Substitution in Turkey,' *Comparative Political Studies*, 22 (1989); or Onis, 'Redemocratization.'
5. Onis, 'Redemocratization,' 10.
6. Barkey, *The State*, pp. 179–81.
7. Ibid., pp. 184–91.

8. Barkey, *The State.*
9. Cited in Andrew Mango, 'The Social Democratic Populist Party, 1983-1989,' in Metin Heper and Jacob Landau (eds), *Political Parties and Democracy in Turkey*, London: I.B. Tauris, 1991, p. 175.
10. Onis, 'Redemocratization,' p. 10.
11. Ibid.
12. John Waterbury, 'Export-led Growth and the Center-right Coalition in Turkey,' in John Waterbury, Teufik Nas and Mehmet Odekon (eds), *Economics and Politics of Turkish Liberalization*, Bethlehem, PA: Lehigh University Press, 1992, pp. 44-72.
13. For a useful categorization of such interests attracted to Ozal, see Barkey, *The State*, p. 178.
14. Tunay, 'The New Turkish Right,' p. 23.
15. Atila Erlap, 'The Politics of Turkish Development Strategies,' in Andrew Finkel and Nukhet Sirman (eds), *Turkish State, Turkish Society*, London: Routledge, 1990, p. 240.
16. Barkey, *The State*, p. 178.
17. Ibid., p. 178.
18. Waterbury, 'Export-led Growth,' p. 65.
19. Ibid.
20. Barkey, *The State*, p. 188.
21. Ibid.
22. Ibid., p. 189.
23. Ustun Erguder in Heper and Landau, *Political Parties*, p. 154.
24. See, for example, *Middle East Economic Digest*, October 14, 1983, 20-21.
25. See, for example, Ahmed Rhazaoui's 'Recent Economic Trends: Managing the Indebtedness,' in I. William Zartman, *The Political Economy of Morocco*, New York: Praeger, 1987.
26. Ibid., p. 152. Also, as a speculative enterprise that considers differences in budget accounting practices, compare Egyptian and Moroccan health, education, and welfare expenditures as a percentage of GNP during the 1980s, in *World Bank Development Reports*, 1980-88. Consistently, such Egyptian expenditures are considerably larger than Moroccan ones – by more that 50 percent in 1980, for example.
27. Rhazaoui, 'Recent Economic Trends,' p. 146.
28. Ibid., p. 144.
29. The Economist Intelligence Unit, *World Outlook, 1984*, London: The Economist, 1984, pp. 117-18.
30. Richard Pomfret, 'Morocco's International Economic Relations,' in Zartman (ed.), *Political Economy of Morocco*, p. 199.
31. Ibid., and *World Development Report, 1987*, p. 244.
32. Rhazaoui, 'Recent Economic Trends,' p. 153.
33. The Economist Intelligence Unit, *World Outlook, 1984*, pp. 117-18.
34. Rhazaoui, 'Recent Economic Trends,' p. 147.
35. Ibid.
36. Ibid., p. 154.
37. Ibid., pp. 154-5.
38. Christian Morrisson, *Adjustment and Equity in Morocco*, Paris: Development Center of the Organization for Economic Cooperation and Development, 1991, p. 115.
39. Alaine Claisse, 'Makhzen Traditions and Administrative Channels,' in Zartman, *Political Economy of Morocco*, p. 45.
40. Clement Henry Moore, 'Political Parties in North Africa,' unpublished paper, October 1990, 7-8.
41. Ibid.
42. Rkia El-Mossadeq in 'Political Parties and Power-Sharing,' in Zartman, *Political Economy of Morocco*, p. 68.
43. Ibid.
44. Mark Tessler, 'Image and Reality in Moroccan Political Economy,' in Zartman, *Political Economy of Morocco*, p. 216.
45. Ibid.
46. Moore, 'Political Parties,' 7.

47. I. William Zartman, 'Opposition as Support of the State,' in Adeed Dawish and Zartman (eds), *Beyond Coercion: The Durability of the Arab State*, London: Croom Helm, 1987, p. 68.
48. Ibid., pp. 66–7.
49. Ibid.
50. Tessler, 'Image and Reality,' pp. 216–17.
51. Zartman in Dawish and Zartman (eds), *Beyond Coercion*, p. 68.
52. I. William Zartman, 'King Hassan's New Morocco,' in Zartman (ed.), *Political Economy of Morocco*, p. 23.
53. Rhazaoui, 'Recent Economic Trends,' p. 141.
54. Daniel Brumberg, 'Prospects for a "Democratic Bargain" in the Middle East,' a paper presented to a National Endowment for Democracy seminar, April 1991, Washington, DC.
55. Robert Springborg, *Mubarak's Egypt*, Boulder, CO: Westview Press, 1989, p. 36.
56. Zartman in Dawish and Zartman (eds), *Beyond Coercion*, p. 76.
57. *The Economist*, April 7, 1984, 65.
58. John Waterbury, 'The "Soft State" and the Open Door: Egypt's Experience with Economic Liberalization, 1974–1984,' *Comparative Politics*, 24 (1991), 68.
59. *The Economist*, April 7, 1984, 65–8.
60. The Economist Intelligence Unit, *World Outlook, 1984*, p. 73.
61. *The Economist*, April 7, 1984, 65.
62. Ibid., March 31, 1984.
63. See my review of the party campaigns in Chapter 4.
64. Richard Moench, 'The May 1984 Elections in Egypt and the Question of Egypt's Stability,' in Linda Layne (ed.), *Elections in the Middle East: Implications of Recent Trends*, Boulder, CO: Westview Press, 1987, p. 52.
65. Ibid.
66. Ibid.
67. *Al Wafd* editorial, May 1984 [in Arabic].
68. I. William Zartman 'Opposition as Support of the State,' in *Beyond Coercion*, pp. 77–9 .
69. Abdul-Reda Assiri and Kamal al-Monoufi, 'Kuwait's Political Elite: the Cabinet,' *Middle East Journal*, no. 42 (1988), 49–50.
70. Ahmad J. Daher and Faisal al-Salem, 'Kuwait's Parliamentary Elections,' *Journal of Arab Affairs*, 3(1) (1984), 85.
71. For example, see Mary Ann Tetreault, 'Autonomy and the Small State: the Case of Kuwait,' *International Organization* (Autumn 1991), 555–91.
72. Daher and al-Salem, 'Kuwait's Parliamentary Elections.'
73. Jill Crystal, *Oil and Politics in the Gulf: Rulers and Merchants in Kuwait and Qatar*, Cambridge: Cambridge University Press, 1990, p. 21.
74. Ibid., p. 36.
75. Ibid., p. 57.
76. Ibid.
77. Jill Crystal, 'Coalitions in Oil Monarchies,' *Comparative Politics* (July 1989), 430–31.
78. Ibid.
79. Tetreault, 'Autonomy and the Small State.'
80. Ibid.
81. Crystal, *Oil and Politics*, p. 85.
82. Ibid., pp. 88–9.
83. *Middle East Economic Digest*, February 27, 1981.
84. Daher and al-Salem, 'Kuwait's Parliamentary Elections,' 95.
85. See ibid. for speculation on overall trends; or for more sophisticated analyses, see Nicolas Gavrielides, 'Tribal Democracy: the Anatomy of Parliamentary Elections in Kuwait,' in Linda Layne (ed.), *Elections in the Middle East: Implications of Recent Trends*, Boulder, CO: Westview Press, 1987.
86. 'Bedouin Eatonswill,' *The Economist*, February 28, 1981.
87. *The Economist*, July 12, 1986.
88. Crystal, *Oil and Politics*, p. 102.

89. See Kamal Osman Salih, 'Kuwait's Parliamentary Elections: 1963–1985: an Appraisal,' *Journal of South Asian and Middle Eastern Studies*, 16(2) (Winter, 1992), 32.
90. 'Tribal Vote Distribution,' *Al Qabbas*, January 12 1985, 1, 4 [Joint Publications Research Service].
91. Salih, 'Kuwait's Parliamentary Elections'; Crystal, 'Coalitions' and Gavrielides, 'Tribal Democracy,' pp. 179–81.
92. Gavrielides, ibid.
93. Ibid.
94. Salih, 'Kuwait's Parliamentary Elections,' 32.
95. Gavrielides, 'Tribal Democracy.'
96. Crystal, *Oil and Politics*, p. 106.

4. Electoral controls and alliances: the position of the business elite and center-right in the parliament

This chapter considers the role of pro-business and center-right groups in the four political openings, and the relations between those groups and the regimes. Here I am particularly interested in the regimes' use of electoral controls to determine the status of these groups in the political system. These mechanisms, I argue, vary somewhat from case to case; however, important commonalities exist across the four political openings. Each regime, in brief, implemented dual strategies of empowerment and exclusion with a fair degree of success.

I argue that common processes of political liberalization exist in the four cases. That is, the government seeks to weaken or strengthen existing parties or factions through a redesign of the electoral or political systems; helps or hinders particular parties or factions by using government resources disproportionately; blocks certain groups from participation altogether; and sometimes sponsors or creates new (dominant) parties. This last and most ambitious option is exercised by the minimally rentier states, since they have been involved in a reorganization of their polities and development models.

Like Dale Eickelman, I assume that an analysis of these forms of government intervention illuminate important political, social, and economic trends.[1] But unlike others interested in political anthropology, who argue that 'seemingly similar' electoral and political institutions have essentially different meanings in different contexts,[2] I am underscoring similarities in the attempts of different regimes to privilege or disadvantage groups of the right and the left. The dynamics of political liberalization, I argue, are roughly comparable across the cases, as each regime copes with the twin pressures of accumulation and legitimation. Members of the liberalizing regime use the tactics of empowerment or exclusion to manufacture popular support for their rule, and to defend the development model considered to be the cornerstone of stable and viable economic growth.

Thus, in this chapter, after describing each regime's electoral controls, I discuss the winners and losers of the process, that is, the coalitions of the right and the left, or more accurately in the Kuwaiti case, the factions representing the relatively privileged and disadvantaged. I discuss the interests of the pro-business and center-right groups, which have important similarities across the cases. That is, in each political opening these groups sought to secure government patronage – to promote the economic interests of big business groups and an upper bourgeoisie. Across the four cases, they sought comparable policies, namely tax rebates, government contracts and subsidies, and, more broadly, a pro-business economic policy that diminished popular-sector entitlements.

Here of course I continue to flesh out my main hypothesis: that the three types of states use such electoral controls to place a center-right bourgeoisie in either a dominant, oppositional, or peripheral parliamentary position.

TURKEY: THE MOTHERLAND PARTY AND THE NEW POLITICAL ELITE

The military's attempt to control the 1983 political opening met with mixed success. True, the regime was unable to create a controlled two-party system based on the dominance of the Nationalist Democracy Party and the 'loyal opposition' of the Populist Party. But it did succeed in its promotion of politicians favoring neoliberalism, and in preventing forces on the left and center-left from disrupting the new political economy. Though unable to guarantee the winners of a semi-competitive polling, the regime was able to shift the ideological bases of the new parliament toward neoliberalism and away from the policies of populism and ISI.

Most important, all three parties permitted to compete in the 1983 poll, including the putatively center-left Populist Party, embraced the stabilization program drawn up by Turgut Ozal in January 1980. Here the junta effectively banned populist platforms from the 1983 elections, as the sanctioned parties all accepted the official reform programs.[3] Further, in banning the precoup politicians and political parties, and curbing the activities of the left and center-left, the military created the electoral and constitutional basis for a vigorous dominance of neoliberal groups during the 1980s and 1990s.

This dominance was, in part, the result of a new electoral system that was designed to strengthen the parliamentary coalition of the party winning a plurality of votes. Consequently, the Motherland Party (MP) received 45 percent of the votes cast, but obtained nearly 53 percent of the parliamentary seats in 1983. Similarly, after pushing an even stronger majoritarian electoral law through the Assembly in 1987, the MP won only 36.3 percent of the votes but almost 65 percent of the seats.[4] Thus, the military regime had anticipated a streamlined right-wing electoral dominance during the 1980s. In the event, however, the MP and not the Nationalist Democracy Party became the beneficiary of the new majoritarian policy, remaining in power until 1991. Observers underscore that the MP's electoral success in 1983 largely resulted from its being the one party that did not appear to be associated with or controlled by the military. Though Ozal had implemented the military regime's economic policies, his resignation in 1982 during a financial scandal and his formation of the MP in 1983 had rankled with the military leadership. Apparently, President Evren's attack on Ozal on television just before the elections increased the MP's popularity. Still, in the first place, the military regime's controls over the electoral process had made the MP the only viable *and* seemingly independent party in the 1983 campaign. That is, among the parties not sponsored by the military, only the MP was permitted to compete. For the junta considered its (pro-orthodox) platform to be acceptable, and the MP was not associated with any pre-1980 parties (which were banned from competition in the 1983 elections).

The Populist Party appeared to have accomplished in the polling what the junta had expected from it: winning 30 percent of the votes, it emerged as the 'center-left' opposition. It perhaps attracted some of the electorate that had previously supported the defunct center-left Republican People's Party.[5] The Populist Party did not hinder the orthodox restructuring process; the junta had not intended that it should do so. Indeed, the party failed to evolve into a relevant political force. The local elections of March 1984 underscored the weakness of both the military-sponsored parties: the Populist Party and the Nationalist Democrats received, respectively, only 9 and 7 percent of the votes cast. The MP again did well, winning about 42 percent of the vote, and demonstrating that it had genuine popular appeal based on economic growth and reform and Islamist traditionalism. Equally important, the Social Democracy Party, in receiving about 24 percent of the vote, trounced the Populist Party in the local elections. Having been banned by the military from the 1983 elections, the Social Democracy Party eventually absorbed the Populist Party and was renamed the Social Democratic Populist Party (SDPP). Subsequently, the SDPP became Turkey's major center-left party. At any rate, the 1984 local elections demonstrated that the 1983 parliamentary elections had provided a weak articulation of interests on the left.[6]

Turgut Ozal and the Rise of the New Right

Scholars underscore the critical continuity in orthodox policies under both the military regime and the Motherland Party administration. The key player throughout the implementation of the policies was Turgut Ozal, who spent a 'formative' period at the World Bank in the mid-1970s, and was the government's main negotiator with international donors during the late 1970s. Ozal, moreover, was the head of a team of high-level technocrats responsible for economic reforms. He was the 'architect' of the January 1980 reform program that was proposed by Demirel's center-right Justice Party and subsequently endorsed by OECD governments and agencies. As such, Ziya Onis observes:

> the Turkish experience provides strong support to the proposition that the character and unity of the technocratic elite, with clear ties to international lending agencies, is a key factor in determining the success of an adjustment program.

Turkey indeed emerged as 'a model during the early 1980s, in terms of the degree of consistency that the policymakers achieved in the implementation of the structural adjustment program.'[7] Though the junta initiated the structural adjustment process, the Motherland Party administration implemented, or followed through on, central aspects of that program: for example, the liberalization of the trade regime, tariff protections, and capital and foreign exchange accounts.[8]

But Ozal's power reflected larger trends in the Turkish political class. More generally, the military's redesign of the electoral process, and the subsequent rise of MP administrations during the 1980s, signified the reconstitution and reorganization of the political elite. Accidental factors helped consolidate the control of this new elite. But the military's effort to reshape the political system was decisive in contributing to the coherence and dominance of the subsequent MP administrations, which remained in power until 1991.

In its attempt to reshape the political system in 1983, the National Security Council not only initiated the formation of two new parties, but banned the participation of the country's veteran politicians and thus prevented the reemergence of the pre-1980 parties. Further, the junta created a blantantly anti-populist constitution and electoral design that blocked the political action of student, union, and other left-wing groups. Finally, the regime permitted only pro-reform parties to contest the 1983 polling.[9] These actions enabled pro-orthodox forces to capture an ascendant position in parliamentary politics.

The banning of the established political elite, writes Yesim Arat, provided businessmen with an unprecedented opportunity to obtain political power. The MP was of course the prime realization of that opportunity. In creating the party, Ozal implored businessmen to enter politics in order to defend their personal interests. Prominent businessmen became the heads of the central party organizations in the major Turkish cities; and a 'network of business links' took control over the party executive. 'To draw businessmen into politics,' Arat concludes, 'was a strategy that Ozal seems to have intentionally promoted and systematically pursued.'[10] With the ban on veteran politicians, and special constitutional and electoral restraints on organization on the left, the era of private sector participation in politics had arrived.

The MP represented the culmination of a trend toward increased political mobility at the elite level. Traditional paths to power had been through the climbing of party hierarchies, and for men hailing from established local families. The rapid development of the postwar era, on Arat's view, had opened avenues of political and economic mobility to individuals from more diverse and peripheral backgrounds. The leaders of the MP, in turn, represented the culmination of this trend toward increased 'upward mobility.' Many of them came from ordinary lower or middle class backgrounds, but almost all had risen to the apex of economic power. Arat observes that:

> working as technocrats, businessmen or both, they [the leaders of the MP] acquired economic power and concomitant prestige. Moving on to the political realm was the next stage in the pursuit of power and status. The wielders of political power in 1983, mostly because of the special circumstances in which they had come to power, had not climbed the ladders of the political hierarchy. Instead, they were moving from elite positions in the socioeconomic realm to elite positions in the political realm.[11]

Ozal succeeded in installing the business elite not just in the party and in the legislature, but in top government positions. For example, 16 of the 22 members of Ozal's first cabinet had held leading positions in the private sector. These ministers had either created new factories or sectors, worked as directors or executives in prominent companies, or had close ties to ENKA Holding, one of Turkey's largest export and construction companies.[12] Arat argues that rapid postwar industrialization somehow made the political rise of this group represented by the MP 'inevitable.'[13] But surely it is easier to trace the rise of the MP to the military's redesign of the political and electoral systems during the early 1980s, as I argue above.

The 1983 MP administration dramatically increased the resources and opportunities available to the private sector. Contrary to some expectations, the shift toward export promotion did not diminish the government's provisions of largesse to private sector groups in the form of credits, concessions, and tax exemptions. The MP administration indeed distributed such provisions among a more diverse array of business groups. Clusters of local industrialists were no longer the primary beneficiaries of government patronage, as had been the case under ISI.[14] A range of new clients, especially in the import-export sector, were able to obtain patronage under the export promotion regime furthered by the MP administration. The new patrons, notes Arat, were typically businessmen and technocrats with links to international markets.[15]

The New Rightist Electoral Coalition

The MP was primarily a party of the business elite and the center-right bourgeoisie, because its ideology focused on their concerns, and because its organizational core and its main beneficiaries were members of these sectors. It was not able, however, to win the semi-competitive 1983 elections without making a broader appeal to the Turkish electorate. The party therefore used an array of ideas and symbols, some of which were inconsistent or disconnected. Indeed, as Ayse Ayata observes, the MP has projected apparently contradictory images: seeming liberal, modern, reformist, pluralist, and anti-bureaucratic; and at the same time, promoting conservative economic, social, and Islamist values, and reflecting 'the rise of a new right in Turkey.'[16] On her view, the central split in the party has been between conservative and traditional Sunni Turks of central Anatolia, and predominantly urban, modernist and upwardly mobile groups. Its ideological appeal, therefore, has been complex, espousing a 'synthesis of modernization and economic growth with safeguards against the fears of the conservative voters who felt threatened by the development program of the party.'[17] Such catchall strategies are of course hardly unusual. Muharrem Tunay, for example, suggests that the MP has resembled Reaganism and Thatcherism in its fusion of 'old' ideas such as moral traditionalism and religious revival, and neoliberal ones such as anti-statism and free markets.[18] In any event, what Ayata sometimes calls mutually exclusive images of the MP in fact have been different facets of a broad and sophisticated electoral strategy.

In the 1983 elections in particular, the MP's catchall appeal apparently resembled that of parties victorious in several founding elections in redemocratizing countries in Latin America. A strong emphasis on civilian rule appealed to some voters of the center and center-left, and orthodox, 'responsible,' and 'modernizing' economic policies appealed to voters on the right. Here commentators underscore the trade-off occurring in redemocratizing countries in the 1970s and 1980s: voters were prepared to forgo populist economic rights in exchange for a stable return to political democracy; and the departing military rulers typically attempted to enhance the standing of conservative parties in the new electoral system.[19] The MP's 1983 victory seems to conform to this pattern, as the party was the only 'non-military' option offered by the National Security Council to an electorate seeking a return to civilian rule.

Once in power, the dynamics of maintaining the MP's electoral coalition became still more complex. As John Waterbury contends, the MP's governing strategy was bifurcated. On the one hand, it supported the large business sector undertaking the export drive. On the other hand, to garner enough votes to stay in power, the MP coalition had to provide significant state largesse to an array of social groups.[20] The party of the Turkish business elite, like its counterparts in Morocco and Egypt, necessarily attempted to accommodate a broad range of electoral concerns, some of which seem disparate or inconsistent. Indeed, the Wafd's 1984 electoral strategy, like that of the MP, focused in part on

Islamist concerns, and attempted to develop a catchall alliance with the Muslim Brotherhood, as discussed below.

In other words, a party representing the business elite tends to absorb other interests as well. My generalizations about business or center-right parties should not obscure this fact. In the Turkish case, one result was the MP's seemingly schizophrenic economic policy and modernist-traditionalist image. In the end, the MP was the main beneficiary of a process that included the reorganization of the political system; the augmentation of the power of the right, especially the export-oriented business sector; the exclusion of the popular sectors from the electoral process; and the implementation of economic programs that were, by Turkish and regional standards, highly austere, orthodox, and anti-populist.

MOROCCO: STREAMLINING THE RIGHTIST ELECTORAL COALITION

The Moroccan regime's reshaping of the political system during 1983–4 was somewhat less sweeping than the Turkish restructuring project of 1982–3. It was, nevertheless, a pivotal episode in Moroccan politics. Of course, the Moroccan regime had more control over the process, since it was engaging in political liberalization and not in (re)democratization. Consequently, unlike the Turkish military's NDP, the crown's preferred party triumphed. But the regime's ability to redefine the political system and close a crisis-ridden chapter in Moroccan politics had been an open question before the 1984 elections. In the end, its electoral controls effectively reorganized the Moroccan political elite and defended the country's new economic directions.

Mustapha Sehimi underscores the diversity and sophistication of the Moroccan state's efforts to strengthen the parliamentary dominance of center-right and pro-orthodox groups. A new tactic was the king's banning of independent candidates in 1984. This prohibition served to preclude the fragmentation of the Popular Movement; to prevent or weaken Islamist and progressive candidates; and to 'oblige tens of cadres' to join the Constitutional Union.[21] Clement Henry Moore notes that the new measure gave royal clients better control over the selection of party candidates, which in turn may have reinforced the cohesion of the parliamentary majority.[22] In any event, the banning of independents signalled the crown's new interest: it now preferred to strengthen the right, and not to pursue its traditional strategy of weakening the parties of both the right and the left through the encouragement of local notables.

More broadly, this requirement of formal political organization represented a restructuring of the polity and resulted from the crown's search for increasingly institutionalized political supports. The king's men *qua* independents dominated the first political openings in the kingdom. Early attempts at royalist parties or electoral associations were 'inept and ineffective,' writes Zartman. Still, he argues, 'the king needed not just men of his own but organizations that supported him.'[23] The RNI was a 'cumbersome and unexciting' attempt to streamline the king's men. The Constitutional Union, in turn, represented a more effective reorganization of the elite. Moreover, it appealed to an electorate that 'was escaping, slipping away from politics and feeling unrepresented by the existing parties.'[24]

Here the monarchy sought to create a dominant electoral force that would be, or appear to be, young and daring: that would engage a disaffected population in the issues of economic (and social) reform. That the new party, organized from above and espousing the conservative ideology of the regime, failed to penetrate society through and through was predictable enough. In concrete terms, notes Sehimi, the creation of the Constitutional Union served to redistribute, but not to increase, the votes for the royalist parties.[25] Its enduring legacy, nevertheless, was the regime's reorganization and formalization of the political elite, as I argue below.

Of course, the regime also used established methods for controlling the elections, namely the gerrymandering of electoral districts, the use of sophisticated technology to doctor electoral results, and the indirect election of one-third of parliament.

As Sehimi observes, the Moroccan government was especially adept at using a 'vast network' of shaiks, moqaddems, and other 'auxiliary agents' of the state to 'discipline the vote of the rural masses.' The regime, therefore, inserted supervised rural districts into urban ones to compensate for the 'fluidity' or volatility of urban voters.[26] One result was that some districts were three or four times as large as other districts, with the largest (Attaouia) having 66 037 voters and the smallest (Tit Mellil-Mediouna) having 14 459 voters. More importantly, the gerrymandering process helped to ensure comfortable victories for the government parties in both the 1977 and 1984 elections, as the electoral system was based on majority voting in single-member constituencies.[27] As Sehimi notes, there was no public outcry against a decree that gerrymandered several districts in August of 1984, on the eve of the polling.[28]

By contrast, during the 1984 campaign, political leaders did complain publicly about the 'quota system,' the formula used by the government to determine the doctoring of electoral results. Before the elections, notes Alain Claisse, government and opposition parties discussed with the Interior Minister their conditions for participation. Only regime insiders knew what the exact distribution of the seats would be. The government did permit the voters to choose some of the seats to give the system 'credibility,' the veneer of democracy.[29]

In the end, on Sehimi's estimate, a truly democratic competition took place for only 51 of 199 of the parliamentary seats contested in the direct elections. In the other constituencies, the regime alloted seats on the basis of royal favor.[30] Electoral fraud and gerrymandering, not to mention the government's control over the media, enabled the crown to fill its electoral quotas in a relatively discrete manner.

But despite its limited indulgence of the USFP in its attempt to legitimate the process, the regime's nurturing of pro-orthodox forces was unmistakable throughout the 1983–4 electoral campaign. Indeed, as Sehimi argues, the quota system was biased against the opposition parties in general and the USFP in particular.[31] That bias was natural enough, since the USFP was the most genuinely popular party and the one most opposed to the regime's development strategy. Like the Istiqlal, it condemned the state's manipulation and falsification of the elections. Nonetheless, with its participation in a national unity government that oversaw the conduct of the 1983–4 campaign, the USFP had become a full participant in, and therefore legitimated, a process that consolidated a royalist and neoliberal parliamentary majority.

Finally, an important feature of the direct elections was a low voter turnout. According to official figures, electoral participation declined from 82.36 percent in 1977 to 67.43 percent in 1984. The turnout was lowest, and the nullification of ballots was highest, in disaffected and pro-socialist urban areas, including those that had experienced the bulk of the civil disturbances occurring in the early 1980s and in January 1984 in particular. These developments reflected a growing militancy and rejection of the electoral system among critical urban segments. Clearly, urban absenteeism reflected a popular belief that the political-electoral system had become 'irrelevant' to some extent. It also seemed to be a response among disaffected sectors to the regime's increasing bias toward the right and its implementation of austere economic policies. In short, they appeared reluctant to cooperate in elections staged by a regime imposing an unpopular economic agenda.[32]

Like those of 1977, the indirect elections of 1984 favored the right-wing government parties. Even among the opposition parties, the regime in 1984 tilted toward the right, giving the Istiqlal 19 seats and the USFP four seats. Here the regime sought to 'restore' the balance between the two opposition parties.[33] Consequently, the Istiqlal remained better represented, even though the USFP was clearly considered the more important force, the one best able to develop links with the masses. The USFP was the third leading vote getter in 1984, but became only the fifth largest party in the parliament. Thus, the party was the big 'loser' in the elections, argued one opposition paper, in the sense that this most popular party occupied the second-to-last spot among 'the gang of six.'[34]

As well, Sehimi notes, the indirect elections heavily favored three royalist parties, in providing the UC with 27 seats, the RNI with 22 seats, and the PND with 15 seats. These parties, in turn, obtained an absolute majority of 154 seats.

Campaign Rhetoric: Royalist Infighting, Isolation of the Left

The leaders of most of the established parties immediately denounced Maati Bouabid for his founding of the UC (the event that unofficially started the electoral campaign in January 1983). His appeal at the founding meeting in Casablanca was ambiguous, calling upon 'eminent civil servants and administrators' to create an 'independent' and 'reformist' party that would organize the post-independence generation and undertake activities 'not permitted' to the other parties.[35] Bouabid then toured important provinces to 'introduce' the party to 'the youth and the cadres.' Observers suggested that it was perhaps 'illogical for the "angry" to leave their parties ... to join one headed by the prime minister.'[36] But the UC's threat to both royalist and opposition parties was clear, as all worried that the new party would steal their votes and greatly diminish the availability of electoral spoils. The UC's broad appeals – to the urban middle classes, disaffected youth, royalists, and the upper bourgeoisie – seemed to target segments of almost every other party's constituency.

The UC was most threatening to the RNI, since those two parties were closest in their consituencies, ideologies, and loyalties to the crown. The RNI also became increasingly critical of government policy, in an attempt to clarify its ideological posturing. Having recently suffered the split from which the PND emerged, the RNI leadership was obviously sensitive to the fact that the UC was intended to be a streamlined replacement of their 'weakening' party.[37] Facing comparable dilemmas, the Popular Movement also expressed strong reservations about the creation of the new party.[38]

As far as the Istiqlal was concerned, the UC was merely another attempt on the part of the regime to manipulate and falsify electoral results. The Istiqlal leader Muhammed Boucetta heaped abuse upon Bouabid, claiming that 'every time there are elections, political parties are formed for one specific purpose: political opportunism and the abuse of power.'[39] The party contrasted its historical nationalist credentials with the recent and seemingly arbitrary advent of the UC. Its attacks on the UC assumed urgency, as its activists realized that the economic crisis and its participation in the government since 1977 had eroded the party's popular base. Consequently, while attacking the UC, the Istiqlal also began to distance itself in vague terms from the development policies of the regime.[40] Nevertheless, the party did not, by and large, emphasize the UC's (or the government's) vision of development. Like the other conservative parties, the Istiqlal focused more on the regime's attempt to pervert the democratic process through the use of 'professionals' who lacked 'all nationalist value' and had 'no popular base.'[41]

Accordingly, for much of the campaign, conservative infighting was considerably more vitriolic than was the jousting between the leftist and conservative parties. Conservative rivals were exorcised by the UC's incursion into a crowded rightist constellation, while the new party did not seem to be a direct threat to the leftist parties. As such, the leftist press focused less on the UC's 'political opportunism' and the 'splintering' of the electorate, and more on the conservatives' ideology and the ramifications of the government's development program.

In response to the Moroccan political and economic crises, the leftist press attempted to present an alternative worldview to that of the conservatives. For example, once authorized in the heat of the campaign to resume publication, the USFP's *Al-Ittihad Al-Ishtiraki* presented broad critiques that attributed Moroccan problems to intertwined crises in the domestic and international capitalist systems. Naturally, the conservative parties would be unable to comprehend the 'full magnitude' of these problems. Moreover, these parties constituted 'a subservient right-wing' that defended the dominant classes' control over both the public and private sectors.[42] In the words of one USFP activist:

> It is a right-wing which expects everything from the government, expects donations, aid, protection, and municipal and parliamentary seats from it; it is a right-wing which is not independent of the administrative system ... It is mercantilist in character economically and it is basically a client by nature politically.[43]

More generally, the USFP called for an end to the flawed export strategies, a break with liberalism and other 'bourgeois ideologies,' and a 'national and democratic revolution' that would effect 'conditions needed to move toward an authentic socialist society.'[44] Such critiques placed the USFP on the periphery of most of the campaign activity, as conservative politicians typically replied that the USFP activists, quite simply, had 'shit for brains.'[45] Though the regime needed the USFP's participation to legitimate the elections, the party remained isolated, rhetorically and ideologically.

The Rise of the UC: Rousing Youth, and Repackaging and Reorganizing the Right

The rhetoric and the reality of the UC were difficult to reconcile. Upon its founding, the party's central theme was, in the words of Sehimi, 'that of the glorification of the participation of youth.'[46] Bouabid claimed that the UC in fact would become a dynamic network, one that would 'lead, guide, and orient' Moroccan youth, and overcome their marginalization, indifference, and hostility. He emphasized that 'it is now the duty of the post-independence generation ... to assume its historic and national responsibilities.' Further, the prime minister suggested that his new party would develop 'organic' and institutionalized links to society: it would be 'a union of the vibrant forces of the nation, one which acts in the framework of constitutional institutions that His Majesty King Hassan II guarantees.'[47]

In the event, despite such appeals for youthful activism, the UC leadership largely depended on, and catered to, the same social segments that had sustained the Moroccan right since independence. Though in fact sending relatively young representatives to parliament in 1984,[48] the UC leadership was drawn from the conservative urban bourgeoisie that monopolized access to King Hassan II. Moreover, the party championed a 'militant' neoliberalism, calling for 'individual initiative,' free enterprise, the development of a liberalized export model, and the privatization of agricultural lands and much of the public sector.[49] What remained unclear was how the party could organize the disaffected masses and, at the same time, embrace such a conservative leadership and ideology.

Bouabid created the UC leadership largely by reshuffling political interests among the royalist parties. His initial organizing efforts focused on regime insiders and leaders and activists of the other royalist parties, particularly the RNI and the PND.[50] The ranks of UC leaders also included prominent urban members of the liberal professions and a range of powerful clients of King Hassan II. This latter group, observes Sehimi, was comprised of landowners, financiers, leaders of economic pressure groups, and the 'personal relations' of royal dignitaries. Men from these circles were primary beneficiaries of the regime's attempt to stimulate the 'private sector;' accordingly, they dominated the UC's ranks of parliamentary deputies candidates.[51]

By and large, the UC leadership was drawn from a bourgeois elite that had long dominated Moroccan politics. That elite, as Mark Tessler observes, has been comprised of:

> the educated sons of the urban bourgeoisie who control the inner circle of national politics and who are the major beneficiaries of high government status. This cadre of elites is socially homogeneous and its bourgeois character reflects a powerful association between political leadership, economic dominance, and privileged origin.[52]

The urban segments of that elite have been particularly cohesive. A network of urban commercial families, the most prominent being the 'thirty or forty sprawling and illustrious'[53] Fassi clans, have dominated Moroccan party politics since independence. Thus, most of the UC leadership revolved around an urban elite sharing privileged origins, a common conservative outlook, and extremely similar educational backgrounds. Local commercial elites apparently assumed a more peripheral status in the new party, though their incorporation was a serious blow to the rural-based PND.

In the end, Bouabid's 'appeal for renewal' signalled the crown's interest in two seemingly irreconcilable objectives. The eminently successful initiative was the streamlining of the nation's bourgeois political elite, who were reorganized in a dominant party that championed neoliberal reform. In forbidding independent candidates, the regime ensured that conservative loyalists would be reorganized within a formal structure espousing the new development program. At the same time, in appealing to young and well-educated members of those same bourgeois families, the creation of the UC was a successful attempt to enliven and professionalize Morocco's dominant political force.

The thoroughly unrealistic objective was the organization of the country's young and disaffected masses, who inevitably were repelled by the new party's conservatism. Of course, the inability of the UC to organize such sectors was always readily apparent. At best, the UC created new and young cadres *within* the urban bourgeois elite.

Nevertheless, such appeals effectively reformulated and repackaged the right and its ideology. Conservative forces rallied around the regime's move toward neoliberal orthodoxy. But the new state ideology, as represented by the UC, at least projected an image of progressive dynamism. In short, regime insiders seemed to claim, a politics of conservatism and royal patronage was becoming a politics of renewal, reform, modernism, and youthful vigor.

In the end, the minimally rentier Moroccan regime, like the Turkish one, had given center-right bourgeois groups an ascendant electoral position. In each case, right-wing groups were best able to exercise the rights of political expression proffered by the political openings in the region's two minimally rentier states. An important distinction between the two reorganization efforts concerns the kinds of bourgeois groups involved in each party. That is, through the MP, newly ascendant segments of the bourgeoisie came to dominate the parliament. By contrast, the UC focused on the reorganization of a bourgeois elite that has dominated the post-independence polity. The crucial commonality, nonetheless, is the fact that each regime embraced the ideology of neoliberalism, and in turn worked to empower bourgeois groups supporting the new anti-populist directions in state development. Likewise, in seeking the rollback of populist and statist structures, each regime ensured the political marginalization of the popular sector.

EGYPT: STREAMLINING A 'POPULIST' MAJORITY AND A BOURGEOIS OPPOSITION, AND ELIMINATING LEFTIST OPPOSITION

Like its Moroccan counterpart, the Egyptian regime deftly organized and controlled the 1984 parliamentary elections. It succeeded in claiming a commanding center-left position for itself, in preventing an oppositional left from winning any parliamentary representation, and in highlighting the importance of a center-right opposition. Also like its Moroccan counterpart, the Egyptian poll worked to consolidate the power of the regime. But unlike the Moroccan crown, the Mubarak regime did not attempt to reorganize the political elite or to legitimate a new economic program. Rather, its election campaign and electoral controls provided a spirited defense of a centrist status quo.

A glance at the five parties' platforms underscores the NDP's interest in the status quo. The two leftist opposition parties called for major policy changes that would reaffirm the interests of the working class; the rightist opposition party demanded the implementation of orthodox reforms. Only the NDP refused to suggest any significant policy changes in the 1984 campaign. As Richard Moench puts it, the regime was banking on a typical pattern of 'growth without development,'[54] that is, growth generated by exogenous revenue.

A new electoral system, passed by the Majlis Al Shaab ('People's Assembly') in the summer of 1983, was crucial in the manufacturing of the desired outcomes in 1984. Elections were now conducted on the basis of proportional representation, with voters choosing national party lists, and parties winning seats in proportion to their votes. Further, electoral districts were reorganized and enlarged. Instead of 175 two-member districts, there were now 48 districts, most having between eight and 14 seats as determined by population size. The old districts had existed with minor changes since 1923. The new system augmented the regime's control over the nomination of candidates.[55] Moreover, the reorganization abetted the NDP and crippled the smaller opposition parties, as the latter did not have sufficient resources for competition in the larger districts. They had hoped to win representation by focusing their efforts on areas of local strength and by leaving areas of party weakness uncontested, as they had done previously.[56]

Finally, and perhaps most importantly, the electoral system required that parties obtain a minimum of 8 percent of the national vote in order to win any seats in parliament. (Parties winning fewer than 8 percent of the national poll forfeited their votes to the frontrunner.) This threshold prevented the two parties left of the NDP from winning parliamentary representation, and effectively ensured that their economic proposals would not be discussed in parliament.[57]

Neither the Socialist Labor Party (*'Amal*) nor the National Progressive Unity Coalition (*Tajammu'*) were especially radical. But both emphasized the rights of the popular sectors in their campaigns, opposed elements of the government's economic reforms, proposed returning the public sector to the center of the country's development strategy; and decried Egypt's dependence on foreign capital and the United States in particular. (*Tajammu'* has had a socialist and Nasirist orientation, and *'Amal* has incorporated nonsocialist pro-union elements.) Both parties complained about the new electoral system, and *Tajammu'* threatened to boycott the elections. When the government began to challenge the legality of the New Wafd, *'Amal* suggested that Wafdists join their party in the event that the New Wafd was banned. But the New Wafd emerged as the strongest opposition party, and hence lost interest in an oppositional alliance, after President Mubarak's intervention ensured that it would be able to compete in the elections. Then, to exceed the 8 percent threshold, *'Amal* and *Tajammu'* began to discuss a joint party list; however, the government promptly decreed that all such joint lists were illegal.[58]

The regime, in sum, ensured that the leftist opposition would be too weak to compete. *Tajammu'* and *'Amal* won 7.02 and 4.17 percent of the vote, respectively. Able to appoint ten parliamentary members, President Mubarak offered each party a token representation. *Tajammu'* rejected Mubarak's offer, and expelled one member who had accepted the President's appointment. The *'Amal* leadership disagreed on whether to accept the token representation; and four members accepted Mubarak's appointment.[59] Both party leaderships considered the 'handouts' to be a humiliating demonstration of their weakness and dependence on the regime. Moreover, the executive appointments would have produced in the case of *Tajammu'*, and did produce in the case of *'Amal*, a truncated parliamentary contingent that was too weak to participate meaningfully in the parliament's 'national dialogue.'

On the right of the spectrum, the re-emergence of the Wafd, whose leaders had been the pre-eminent politicians of the pre-1952 era, must be attributed to a personal decision by President Mubarak to tolerate the rehabilitation of the party, contrary to the desires of much of the NDP. Clearly, in the spring of 1984, he had the opportunity to side with those government members seeking the banning of the party. As I argue in the section below, economic pressures and the unique resources of the national bourgeoisie ultimately compelled the regime to permit the New Wafd to participate, and as the sole oppositional force in the parliament. Meanwhile, the emergence of the New Wafd as the national party of the bourgeoisie made the Liberal (*Ahrar*) Party, as Moench puts it, 'totally redundant.'[60] Regime loyalists had created the Liberal Party in the 1970s to give Sadat's political opening a more pluralistic veneer. In 1984, the core Liberal Party members defected to the New Wafd after it became clear that the latter was able to compete and had the best chance of exceeding the 8 percent threshold. (Consequently, the Liberals won less than 1 percent of the vote.) In sum, the Mubarak regime permitted an effective aggregation and representation of interests on the oppositional right, but prohibited as much on the oppositional left.

The Rise of the New Wafd

That the New Wafd won 15.2 percent of the vote and 58 parliamentary seats signalled that the regime wanted to achieve an accommodation with oppositional forces that was unprecedented in the post-1952 era. Under Sadat, Majlis Al Shaab elections typically produced lilliputian oppositions, which in any event were dominated by regime loyalists pretending to be in opposition. In 1976, for example, putatively oppositional 'platforms' won only 14 seats. In 1979, Sadat created the Socialist Labor Party and told NDP members to run on the *'Amal* list. The party won 28 seats that year, but half of those deputies then defected back to the NDP.[61] By contrast, the New Wafd was always an independent entity – indeed, one that had once dominated the polity and had subsequently been attacked by the Nasirist regime. Members of the Wafd's 'old guard' had particularly bitter memories of the persecution and wealth sequestrations under Nasir; and during the campaign, both new and old Wafdists alike railed against the NDP's corruption and disastrous political, economic, and social policies.[62] They were, in sum, entirely hostile toward the regime, calling for its downfall and for the New Wafd's rightful assumption of, or return to, power. Thus, in 1984, the regime's indulgence of the opposition – that is, the rightist opposition – was qualitatively and quantitatively unprecedented.[63]

The NDP and the New Wafd offered, despite important commonalities, substantially different visions of socioeconomic development during the campaign. A dominant NDP theme, one of 'paramount importance,' as one *Al-Ahram* editorial put it in late April, was the maintenance of social justice, production prices, and subsidies.[64] A few days later, the leading government newspapers promised that the NDP would continue to subsidize 'all essential goods,' lest prices fluctuate radically.[65] Repeatedly, the government press highlighted the NDP's commitment to the provision of services and welfare to the popular sectors, and claimed that subsidies and wages had risen dramatically since 1980. (For example, Dr Fouad Mohieddin, the Prime Minister and the NDP General Secretary, boasted that wages had increased by 252 percent during the last three years, and that subsidies had risen from LE 622 million since 1975 to LE 2053 million in 1984.[66]) More generally, the NDP called for a 'democratic socialism'[67] that would invigorate and build upon the Nasirist achievements and protect them from the onslaught of conservative or reactionary forces, be they the New Wafd or the IMF.

Despite such charges from the NDP, Wafdists attempted to offer a guarded and balanced, if highly critical, assessment of the July 26 Revolution. (A typically defensive *Al-Wafd* editorial was entitled 'Yes to the Positives ... and No to the Negatives.'[68]) The principal charges of the New Wafd during 1984 concerned the Revolution's corrupt and authoritarian legacies as manifested in the NDP. Somewhat less strident, but nevertheless important was the party's call for orthodox economic reforms, particularly the dismantling of the bloated public sector. Both the NDP and the New Wafd claimed they supported variants of a 'productive *infitah*.' But while the NDP continued to emphasize welfarism and etatism, the New Wafd asserted that the 'economic freedom' of both workers and employers was only realizable in the private sector, outside the sphere of government control. Only free-market reforms and a rollback of the Nasirist state structures, the party claimed, could cure Egypt of its economic stagnation and perpetual underdevelopment.[69]

Despite its condemnation of the elections as an utter fraud, the New Wafd claimed that it had achieved a tremendous victory. It congratulated itself heartily on having opened 'the doors of parliament.'[70] Moreover, what the regime's electoral design implied the New Wafd said outright: that legitimate Egyptian political discourse had evolved into a struggle between the two parties, or, at any rate, between their two visions. The New Wafd claimed that it had become the only national alternative, and that it indeed was poised to win the next *free* elections! (One editorial even claimed incorrectly that the British press, especially *The Economist*, expected its victory in the next elections.[71]) Rhetoric aside, the elections had signaled that the NDP had conceded an unprecedented role of legitimate opposition to the center-right and the business elite through the New Wafd. The election results permitted the New Wafd and the regime to make similar claims: namely, Egyptians faced a choice between NDP-style welfarism and Wafd-style neoliberalism.

Structuring Class Participation in Politics

Observers point to the indifference of much of the population to the 1984 elections. The government reported a voter turnout of only 43 percent, and it is estimated that roughly 80 percent of the urban electorate did not vote.[72] Indeed, throughout the 1980s and 1990s, while claiming to be the voice of the Egyptian working class, the NDP did not seek its political mobilization. (For example, the Mubarak regime demobilized and deactivated much of the trade union movement as a corporatist political force.[73]) The regime's goal seems to have been the cultivation of the popular sectors' passive acceptance of NDP rule.

Why did the regime simultaneously promote the active political participation of a center-right bourgeoisie? Interrelated factors have prompted the regime to seek the involvement of such groups in its political-economic program. First, it has sought to encourage such groups to cooperate with, and provide capital for, the regime's development programs. Indeed, their resources and cooperation were essential to the regime's mildly reformist economic program during the 1980s.[74] Second, the economic cooperation of the center-right has had a political price; for center-right groups, through the New Wafd, have been perhaps the most strident proponents of increased political liberalization and democratization. Consequently, the Mubarak regime has attempted to develop a political strategy that would coopt and accommodate these groups within the processes of political and economic reform.[75]

In brief, Egypt *qua* semi-rentier state sought an accommodation with these groups because they possess resources essential to the regime's development program, and because these resources give them the wherewithal to disrupt the regime's political-economic programs. These business groups, in dominating the *infitah* bourgeoisie, had strong ties to Western capital. They include, for example, 5000 agents of foreign firms, 7500 import agents, and powerful political and business leaders who have openly sided with and advocated the policies of USAID. Many of these leaders were NDP supporters. But after 1984, the electoral voice representing their views on development was the oppositional one of the New Wafd.

Simultaneously, the decline of ISI economies throughout the Third World, and the concomitant development of an orthodox macroeconomic consensus among the international financial community, have had a powerful impact on the political-economic development of semi- and minimally rentier states in general. As I explained in Chapter 1, the Egyptian government has received powerful international incentives during the 1980s and 1990s to create a political system that hinders the political effectiveness of popular-sector groups, and promotes and legitimates groups associated with efficient and export-oriented economic activity. Apparently, the regime calculated that popular mobilization was too risky, given the hegemonic global orthodoxy. It has nonetheless been vulnerable to popular demands, and unlike its Moroccan and Turkish counterparts, it has had more resources to cater to them.

In sum, access to substantial amounts of exogenous rents enabled the Egyptian state to maintain a limited populism, and to avoid any real empowerment of center-right groups, or any real adoption of a center-right development strategy. More generally, John Waterbury has called the Egyptian state 'soft' in the sense that it is vulnerable to the economic demands of the popular sectors. 'Easy money,' he wrote in 1984, has made possible a 'softhearted' Egyptian authoritarianism.[76] But from the perspective of my framework, the key factor during these years of Third World economic austerity has been the regime's ability, albeit with increasing difficulty, to continue to cater to these popular demands. In the end, the regime has been able to maintain a balance between orthodox and heterodox policies; and in turn, its concessions to the center-right have been limited.

A Word about Islamist Groups

One unexpected consequence of the electoral accommodation with the center-right was the rehabilitation of the Muslim Brotherhood as a *de facto* and yet legitimate player within the electoral system during the 1984 and 1987 campaigns. Technically banned since 1954, the Egyptian Brotherhood existed on the political margins during the 1960s and early 1970s. At the same time, many of their activists and leaders assumed prominent positions in giant Gulf-based multinational corporate, investment and banking conglomerates. With the advent of Sadat's 'open door' policy in the mid-1970s, Brotherhood leaders began to channel significant amounts of Gulf capital into Egypt; and Sadat offered the organization *de facto* recognition, as he enlisted its support in countering his left-wing rivals. At the same time, Brotherhood participation in Sadat's electoral experiments remained highly circumscribed, and by 1981 Sadat repressed the organization, fearing its rising popularity and citing its opposition to his visit to Jerusalem and the Camp David Accords, among other things.[77]

Under Mubarak, the Brotherhood made a dramatic, albeit *de facto*, re-entry into the normative confines of the political system. The regime did not legalize the Brotherhood, but the organization was able to accept the New Wafd's invitation to join its electoral list for the 1984 elections. Eight of the New Wafd's 58 successful candidates were Brotherhood members. At first glance, the New Wafd–Brotherhood alliance was a strange marriage of secular and religious interests. Some argue that the Brotherhood and the New Wafd's 'old guard' shared a vendetta against the regime's 'lingering Nasirist influence,' a passion more powerful than their respective interests in secularism and Islamism.[78] Secularist party members protested the alliance, and the New Wafd's platform only made token references to the application of shari'a. Not surprisingly, the alliance proved to be tactical and short-lived. After the elections, the Brotherhood parliament members abandoned the coalition in an attempt to take over the tiny *Ahrar* and *Umah* parties.[79] The Brotherhood then did well in the 1987 parliamentary elections through an alliance with the *Ahrar* and *'Amal* parties. But concerning their development ideologies, the New Wafd–Brotherhood alliance was oddly appropriate, for the two organizations shared an interest in neoliberalism; and the regime sought a comparable political-economic accommodation with both organizations during the 1980s.

The Brotherhood's conceptualization of economic development experienced a transformation during the 1970s and 1980s. Having jettisoned its pro-welfarism of the Nasirist period, the Brotherhood's leadership, by and large, became a champion of neoconservatism. According to an *Al-Ahram* survey, the Brotherhood members of parliament during the 1980s were considerably more conservative than their NDP counterparts and every bit as conservative as those of the New Wafd. For example, they called for the mass privatization of the public sector; stressed the importance of the defense of private property; supported the altering of tenancy laws to favor owners; had little interest in illiteracy and the plight of the peasantry; and claimed that the private sector was in the best position to resolve pressing socioeconomic issues such as the housing crisis.[80]

The new macroeconomics of a moderate Islam apparently had a useful oppositional role to play in the Egyptian parliament. It seems, in sum, quite reasonable to speculate that economic pressures strongly encouraged the Egyptian regime to find an electoral accommodation giving the Brotherhood – especially one that had shed its radical image, and had powerful links to international Islamic banking and investment networks – a legitimate voice in the political system. The upshot is that the orientation of electoral politics toward the cooptation of the bourgeoisie has had a powerful impact not only on the secular opposition, but on the rise of a more 'mainstream' Islamist movement during the mid- and late-1980s, as led by the Brotherhood.

KUWAIT: THE RISE OF THE DISADVANTAGED, THE DECLINE OF THE UPPER BOURGEOISIE

The Kuwaiti electoral experiment of the 1980s reflected the regime's efforts to create a dominant electoral coalition through the consolidation of Beduin parliamentary power. In this sense, the Kuwaiti project resembled the Moroccan and Turkish ones, with each attempting to restructure the political system. Of course, the highly and the minimally rentier regimes were moving their polities in opposite directions: the latter sought to empower the upper bourgeoisie and weaken the popular sectors; the former attempted to weaken the upper bourgeoisie and empower a disadvantaged Beduin sector, which is in the Kuwaiti case sometimes called the 'popular' sector.

In turn, these three cases differ from the Egyptian one in that the Mubarak regime only sought to reorganize the opposition, and did not seek to restructure the ruling coalition or the opportunities for participation at the political center. Here the Egyptian regime's relatively stagnant approach reflected its desire to balance the pressures of the right and the left. The

Kuwaiti approach, in contrast, dealt with much broader trends, including, most importantly, the demographic restructuring of the polity.

The Rise of the Beduin

The Al Sabah family's central mechanisms of electoral control have revolved around the issues of citizenship, patronage, and redistricting. Comprised in 1981 of roughly 90 000 potential voters – that is, male citizens over the age of 21 – the polity is tiny, and is therefore vulnerable to attempts at demographic redefinition. As I discuss in Chapter 3, the Al Sabah family's chief political rival in the pre-oil era had been the 'merchant' families that have comprised the country's business elite. The regime has worked to diminish the political clout of the merchant families by creating a new group of citizens who would be hostile to the entrenched political power of the business elite.

Nicolas Gavrielides has underscored the relationship between the regime's parliamentary strategy and the granting of citizenship only to the Beduin. During the oil era, citizenship has been granted to large numbers of Beduin tribesmen, but denied to virtually all other groups, be they Arab or non-Arab. Reportedly, the key hurdle to citizenship has been an interview with a 'citizenship committee,' which tests the authenticity of the applicant's claim to tribal background.[81] The government has been especially well-disposed toward applications from those members of Beduin tribes considered particularly loyal to the Al Sabah. In turn, the government has given new citizens jobs, especially in the police or military, and provided them with housing in special Beduin-only suburbs. These segregated neighborhoods were particularly important in the regime's 1981 redistricting project, as discussed below.

The goal of the government during the oil era, Gavrielides concludes, has been 'to provide control over the army and a check on the merchants, the Liberal/Leftists, the Fundamentalists, and the Shia through the use of [Beduin] tribesmen.'[82] The issue of citizenship, he argues, is 'intimately related' to the regime's attempt to tribalize the political system, and to weaken the merchant elite and other Kuwaiti factions. This policy in fact became an important campaign issue during the 1980s, as members of the liberal/leftist and merchant blocs engaged in pointed attacks on the government's policy. They complained about the giving of citizenship to non-productive (Beduin) 'outsiders,' about the relegating of many urban Kuwaitis to a second-class, nonvoting citizenship, and about the government's reshaping of Kuwait's demographic balance.[83]

Through the Beduin, observes Gavrielides, the ruling family has assumed its 'ultimate ideal role'[84] of *muazib*, or patron, in the building of the pro-Sabah Beduin parliamentary order of the 1980s. The Al Sabah family has expected loyalty from those groups, particularly the Beduin, who benefit from welfare provisions. Conversely, the families of the economic elite have shunned those services. They do not have much need for the services, but moreover wish to maintain their independence from the state and to distinguish themselves from the relatively disadvantaged Kuwaiti groups.

The result was that the regime created a sharp confrontation between Beduins and the merchant elite in the 1981 and 1985 elections. Here tribal and class identities came to reinforce one another. The merchant and liberal/leftist groups, notes Gavrielides, felt 'outnumbered and out-manuevered by the naturalization of [Beduin] tribesmen.' The merchants' resentment toward the new citizens had increased during the 1970s, as 'the Beduin and their dependents [were] in their view non-productive – refusing to perform any productive labor but demanding services which necessitate the importation of foreigners.'[85]

Complementing the use of patronage and the creation of a new citizenry was the regime's redistricting project of 1980. Ten voting districts, each sending five representatives to the National Assembly, were used during the first four parliamentary elections (1963, 1967, 1971, and 1975). In 1981, the regime divided the ten districts into 25 districts, each with two deputies instead of five. In turn, seats in predominantly Beduin districts increased from 25 to 31; seats in predominantly Shi'a districts decreased from twn to four; and seats in the predominantly urban districts remained at 15.

The strengthening of the electoral dominance of the Beduins during the 1980s was, in effect, the regime's response to its loss of control over the leading parliamentary groups during the mid-1970s. At the time of its dissolution in 1976, the National Assembly had become the focal point of an increasingly vocal and diverse opposition. The Al Sabah suspended the body, in large part, because of the collapse of the dominant electoral coalition of Beduins, Shi'a and Sunni groups. With the onset of the Iranian Revolution and of Shi'a unrest in Kuwait during the fall of 1979, the regime sought to increase its support among Kuwaiti nationals, to sharpen the distinction between Kuwaiti nationals and expatriate residents, and to prevent the importation of revolutionary Islamist contagion through the reinstatement of the Assembly.

Though 447 candidates competed for 50 Assembly seats, the regime carefully controlled the 1981 opening. Most important, it gerrymandered 25 electoral districts to disadvantage Shi'a groups, and to promote Beduin and sectarian allies.[86] An increase in the overrepresentation of Beduins, who won 28 seats, was the principal outcome of the 1981 election. As a relatively small Kuwaiti minority, they had controlled, on one estimate, roughly 50 percent of the seats in the four previous parliaments. Though this overrepresentation had fueled a Beduin–urban rivalry in the previous Assembly, the regime abetted the increase of Beduin members to 56 percent through the creation of additional electoral districts in rural areas. The 1981 Assembly also included six Sunni Islamists, three Arab nationalists, and two Shi'as. Having controlled roughly 20 percent of the seats during the previous four Assembies, the Shi'as were the biggest losers in 1981. They were now underrepresented, while Beduins and Sunni Islamists accounted for more than two-thirds of the Assembly members.

The 1981 and 1985 elections accelerated the long-term decline of the parliamentary power of the leading merchant families. They won only two seats in each of these elections, having obtained 12 seats in 1963, eight seats in 1967, seven seats in 1971, and six seats in 1975.[87]

In the end, and unlike the electoral experiments in the semi- and minimally rentier states, the Kuwaiti opening of 1981 was not designed to offer bourgeois groups a powerful and distinctive role in parliamentary politics. Though they had represented the most important political power after the royal family during the pre-oil era, the regime's controls over the electoral process had reduced them to one of several rivals in the Assembly and in political life in general.

Gavrielides concludes that the Kuwaiti parliament has been one 'in which the tribal element contains the merchants who seek more power from the rulers, the Liberal/Left which seeks social and economic equality, and the Fundamentalists who seek an Islamic government.'[88] Gavrielides acknowledges that this outcome corresponded with the wishes of the ruling family, but concludes that 'direct' government interference in the electoral process was not central to the Beduin victory. He ultimately attributes tribal–Beduin dominance during the 1980s to the citizens' appreciation and acceptance of government efforts to structure and legitimate social and political life on a tribal basis. A tribal–Beduin parliamentary predominance, he argues, represents a harmonious fusion of Western political institutions and 'indigenous' traditions.[89] This conclusion is particularly odd, given his convincing claims that the government's policies of citizenship, patronage, and redistricting effectively reshaped the Kuwaiti polity in the post-independence era. After all, the Kuwaiti merchant families, like the Beduin, are also tribe members whose political participation has been oriented around overlapping class and tribal interests. Apparently, as Kamal Osman Salih observes, the rising power of the Beduins in the 1980s was in part due to their 'aggressive [electoral] campaigns' calling for the provision of essential services to their constituencies.[90] But at bottom, through the redesign of the polity and electoral system, the regime provided the electoral and political structures that effected a decisive shift of political power from the merchants to the Beduins.

Further, it is difficult to reconcile the reality of an essentially non-Beduin

Kuwaiti society with Gavrielides' praise for the Kuwaiti parliamentary system and for the Beduin dominance of parliamentary politics in particular. Indeed, it seems that contradictions between an essentially non-Beduin Kuwaiti citizenry and a Beduin-dominated parliament have, to an extent, delegitimated the National Assembly. This discrepancy has caused the core urban elite and middle class to be less inclined to defend the parliament from the predations of the ruling family.

Redistricting and the Shifting Tribal Balance: the Coincidence of Class and Ethnicity in the 1981 Elections

In January 1985, a series of articles analyzing the impact of redistricting on the 1981 polling was published by *Al Qabbas*, a daily Kuwaiti newspaper owned by one of the most prominent merchant families. Using data from the Ministry of Planning and the Central Statistics Administration, the authors of the series underscore that the new districts reinforced overlapping ethnic and socio-economic voting patterns. Like Crystal, Salih, and Gavrielides, they assert that the 1980 redistricting increased the number of Beduin deputies, decreased the number of Shi'a deputies, and maintained those from the urban/Sunni districts at their 1975 level. But in using 1980 census data, the *Al Qabbas* study also illustrated the extent to which overlapping ethnic and socioeconomic identities had come to dominate the electoral process.

The new and increasingly stratified districts, in part, reflected 'new demographic concentrations,' but moreover resulted from an 'intentional and premeditated' attempt to reorder the tribal and sectarian balance.[91] Like Gavrielides and Crystal, the *Al Qabbas* writers pointed to the increase in the number of districts in outlying Beduin areas. As well, they noted that, by increasing the number of districts from 10 to 25, and by reducing the number of deputies in each district from five to two, the regime was able to ensure that the new districts would in all likelihood produce deputies who only represented the ethnic or sectarian majority therein.

Further, the authors argue that 1980 census data confirmed that the redistricting played on socioeconomic divisions in addition to the ethnic-sectarian ones. They focused much of their analysis on the governates of Al Asima, Al Jahra, and Al Ahmadi, which contained 15 of the 25 electoral districts. An urban Sunni constituency dominated the Al Asima ('Capital') district; Beduins predominated in the outlying Al Jahra and Al Ahmadi districts; and only the fifth district of Kafyan had a mixture of Beduins and Sunni urbanites. The ten districts of the fourth and largest governate of Al Hawalli contained large concentrations of all three major groupings (Sunnis, Shi'as, and Beduins).

The census found that 52.1 percent of the potential voting population (adult male citizens) were illiterate or could barely read or write. These people comprised roughly two-thirds of the voters in the mainly Beduin Al Jahra and Al Ahmadi, but only 9.8 percent of the predominantly Sunni Al Asima. Conversely, of the 5495 college graduates (5.3 percent of the voting population), roughly 90 percent lived in the Al Asima and Al Hawalli, and 10 percent lived in Al Jahra and Al Ahmadi. Similarly, about 81 percent of the potential voters with high school or 'sub-college' degrees lived in Al Asima or Al Hawalli, while 19 percent were from Al Jahra and Al Ahmadi.

Likewise, the vast majority of the Al Asima voters were engaged in what the census had designated the top four technical or administrative professions, which tended to yield comparatively high salaries. By contrast, most voters from Al Jahra and Al Ahmadi had the relatively low-paying jobs that the census included in the bottom three employment categories. In a word:

> the new redivision has led to the concentration of the groups with the higher incomes, education, and professions in the model [Sunni/urban] districts and the concentration of the groups with the lower incomes, education levels and professions in the outer [Beduin] districts.

Consequently, they conclude, the redistricting damaged 'national unity' and augmented 'the sectarian–tribal action of the traditional political groupings.'[92]

Merchants and the Changing Polity

The *Al Qabbas* writers, like Crystal and Gavrielides, suggest that the regime had no interest in giving the Kuwaiti bourgeoisie an important and distinctive political role. Merchant leaders railed against the escalation of 'tribalism,' but in the end seemed more dismayed that they had been pushed into a peripheral role in the evolving polity. The merchant faction, after all, had moral and historical claims to political dominance. Beduins did not even have such claims to citizenship, let alone predominance in the parliament. In an interview published in *Al Mujtama*, Abd Al Aziz Al Saqr, the President of the Chamber of Commerce and one of Kuwait's foremost merchants, remarked that 'the most blatant' error in modern Kuwaiti history was 'the [Beduin] citizenship policy' of the early 1960s and 1970s. The country was still

> reaping the bitter fruit of this policy, which arose from purely political motives and did not, in my opinion, have any justification. The most dangerous of these fruits have been tribal ideology and factional fanaticism.[93]

The merchants now were resigned to their reliance on quieter and informal mechanisms, such as the Chamber of Commerce. Thus, Al Saqr observed that:

we have not withdrawn from political activity. Rather, we have withdrawn from political action, one of whose most important activities is considered to be membership in the National Assembly.

None of the merchants, he added, 'would stint in offering his counsel' whenever necessary.[94] Chamber of Commerce policy pronouncements, on issues such as the provision of government contracts to leading Kuwaiti (merchant) firms instead of foreign ones, were typical of the new kinds of 'political activity.'

CONCLUSION

The Kuwaiti electoral process of the 1980s demonstrates how the regime enabled a socioeconomically disadvantaged sector to eclipse what had been one of Kuwait's traditional political powers. As the minimally rentier regimes worked to streamline the electoral capabilities of pro-business and pro-orthodox bourgeois groups, the highly rentier regime sought to streamline the power of a traditionally disadvantaged, or 'populist,' tribal–Beduin sector.

Of the four cases, the Kuwaiti one was unique in that the regime did not give the upper bourgeoisie an important and distinct parliamentary role, either in the majority or in the opposition. At the same time, all four regimes used comparable, if not identical, tactics to strengthen or weaken particular groups. The Moroccan, Egyptian, and Kuwaiti regimes, for example, all used redistricting to ensure preferred electoral outcomes.

Finally, this chapter shows that the democratizing Turkish regime was less able to dictate the results of the electoral process than were the relatively authoritarian Arab ones. In the Arab cases, the regimes were successful in installing their preferred party or faction (though in the Kuwaiti case, that faction eventually turned against the government in 1986). The Turkish regime succeeded in conducting a poll that protected its orthodox development program, though it did not succeed in installing the party it had created. Nevertheless, the Turkish military was able to improve the parliamentary interests of an upper bourgeoisie and a pro-orthodox center-right in general. In this sense, the Turkish regime, like the Arab ones, did succeed in its redesign of the polity.

NOTES

1. Dale Eickelman, 'Royal Authority and Religious Legitimacy: Morocco's Elections, 1960–1984,' in Myron J. Aronoff, *The Frailty of Authority*, New Brunswick, NJ: Transaction Books, 1986, pp. 181–206.

2. This is, for example, Linda Lanyne's assumption in her summary of regional electoral trends, in L. Layne (ed.), *Elections in the Middle East: Implications of Recent Trends*, Boulder, CO: Westview Press, 1987, p. 14.
3. *Middle East Economic Digest*, October 14, 1983, 20–21.
4. Clement Henry Dodd, *The Crisis of Turkish Democracy*, 2nd edn, Wistow, Cambs: Eothen Press, 1990, p. 98.
5. Ustun Erguder and Richard I. Hofferbert, 'The 1983 General Elections in Turkey: Continuity or Change in Voting Patterns,' in Metin Heper and Ahmet Evin (eds), *State, Democracy, and the Military: Turkey in the 1980s*, Berlin: Walter de Gruyter, 1988, p. 98.
6. Ibid.
7. Ziya Onis, 'Redemocratization and Economic Liberalization in Turkey: the Limits of State Autonomy,' *Studies in Comparative International Development*, 27(2) (1992), 10–11.
8. Ibid.
9. See my discussion on pp. 25–6 in Chapter 2.
10. Yesim Arat, 'Social Change and the 1983 Governing Elite in Turkey,' in Mubeccel Kiray (ed.), *Structural Change in Turkish Society*, Bloomington, IN: Indiana University Turkish Studies, 1991, p. 168.
11. Ibid., p. 166.
12. Ibid., p. 168.
13. Ibid., p. 169.
14. Ibid.
15. Ibid.
16. Ayse Ayata, 'Ideology, Social Bases, and Organizational Structure,' in Atila Erlap, Muharrem Tunay, and Birol Yesilada (eds), *The Political and Socioeconomic Trans-formation of Turkey*, Westport, CT: Praeger, 1993, p. 33.
17. Ibid., pp. 33–9.
18. Muharrem Turay, 'The New Right's Attempt at Hegemony,' in Erlap *et al.* (eds), *Political and Socioeconomic Transformation*, p. 16.
19. Nancy Bermeo, 'Rethinking Regime Change,' *Comparative Politics*, 22(3) (1990), 359–77.
20. John Waterbury, 'Export-led Growth and the Center-right Coalition in Turkey,' in John Waterbury, Tevfik Nas and Mehmet Odekon (eds), *Economics and Politics of Turkish Liberalization*, Bethlehem, PA: Lehigh University Press, 1992, p. 45.
21. Mustapha Sehimi, 'Les elections legislatives au Maroc,' *Maghreb-Machrek*, no. 107 (1985), 33.
22. Clement Henry Moore, 'Political Parties in North Africa,' unpublished conference paper, October 1990, 5.
23. I. William Zartman, 'King Hassan's New Morocco,' in I.W. Zartman (ed.), *The Political Economy of Morocco*, New York: Praeger, 1987, p. 27.
24. Ibid.
25. Sehimi, 'Les elections,' 27.
26. Ibid., p. 25.
27. Moore, 'Political Parties,' 5.
28. Ibid.
29. Alain Claisse, 'Makhzen Traditions,' in Zartman (ed.), *Political Economy of Morocco*, p. 46.
30. Sehimi, 'Les elections,' 39.
31. Ibid., pp. 42–3.
32. Ibid., p. 37.
33. Ibid., p. 43.
34. Zakya Daoud, 'A New Political Geography,' *Lamalif*, no. 159 (October 1984), 4–5 [Joint Publications Research Service].
35. 'Bouabid Announces the Formation of a New Party,' *Al Destour*, January 24, 1983, 26–7 [Joint Publications Research Service].
36. 'Morocco Living in Partisan Card-shuffling Period,' *Al Ra'y*, February 4, 1983, 8–9 [Joint Publications Research Service].
37. 'Bouabid Announces,' *Al Destour*.
38. Ibid.

39. Ibid.
40. Ibid.
41. Ibid.
42. 'Excerpts from Fathallah Lahlou's Address to the 5th Meeting of Union Youth in Maamoura,' *Al Ittihad, Al Ishtiraki*, April 19 1984: 5 and April 21 1984: 3, 5.
43. Ibid.
44. Ibid.
45. Cited in Zartman, 'King Hassan's New Morocco.'
46. Mustapha Sehimi, *La Grande Encyclopédie du Maroc: les institutions politiques*, Rabat: GEM, 1985, p. 102.
47. Ibid.
48. Sehimi, 'Les elections,' 45.
49. Sehimi, *La Grande Encyclopédie*, p. 103.
50. Sehimi, 'Les elections,' 42.
51. Bouabid also cultivated links between the UC and the Moroccan Federation of Labor, the country's most powerful union. In having long-standing ties to the organization, the Prime Minister seemed, in the words of one journalist, to be creating 'a rightist party ... claiming to defend the workers' (Waterbury, quoted in Mark Tessler, 'Institutional Pluralism and Monarchical Dominance,' in I. William Zartman (ed.), *Political Elites in Arab North Africa*, New York: Longman, 1982).
52. Tessler, 'Institutional Pluralism'.
53. 'Bouabid Announces,' *Al Destour*, 27.
54. Richard Moench, 'The May 1984 Elections in Egypt and the Question of Egypt's Stability,' in Layne, *Elections in the Middle East*, p. 52.
55. Ibid., p. 57.
56. Ibid., p. 55.
57. Ibid., p. 57.
58. Ibid., p. 58.
59. Ibid., p. 57.
60. Ibid., p. 68.
61. Like *Tajammu'*, *'Amal* was originally formed by the regime, but gradually became increasingly independent. They were both in essentially hostile opposition by the 1984 elections.
62. See, for example, the *Al Wafd* editorials (in Arabic) of March and April 1984.
63. Surely, that indulgence was also thoroughly purposive. As one scholar argues, the Egyptian regime's electoral authoritarianism is typical in the Middle East, in that election results are essentially a reflection of the desires of the rulers, and not of popular sentiment. Computerization of the vote-tallying, in addition to all the other electoral controls, has made the Egyptian regime infamous for its ability and desire to fine-tune the results of the polling (see, for example, the editorial in *Al Wafd*, June 7, 1984). Of course, concerning democratization and the conduct of the elections, the NDP and New Wafd also offered wildy contrasting programs and interpretations: for example, the NDP declared that the elections were a 'momentous historical event' and the most democratic in decades (see lead story in *Al-Ahram*, May 24, 1984); the New Wafd considered the elections to have been a sham (see, for example, the lead story, ibid., April 26, 1984).
64. See James A. Bill and Robert Springborg, *Politics of the Middle East*, 3rd edn, New York: HarperCollins, 1990, p. 291.
65. See the lead story, *Al Gomhuriya*, April 21, 1984.
66. Lead story, *Al-Ahram*, May 24 1984.
67. Ibid., April 21, 1984, 1.
68. Mona Makram Abaid, 'Yes to the Positives ... and No to the Negatives,' *Al Wafd* (in Arabic), July 19, 1984, 6.
69. See, for example, Ibrahim Dessouki Abaza, 'The state ... a private sector!' *Al Wafd* (in Arabic), November 1, 1984, 6.
70. See Abaza, 'Congratulations, Wafd,' *Al Wafd* (in Arabic), June 7, 1984, 3.
71. Mustapha Al Bahairi, 'Reactions to the Elections in Britain,' *Al Wafd*, June 14, 1984, 10.

72. Moench, 'The May 1984 Elections,' p. 49.
73. Robert Springborg, *Mubarak's Egypt*, Boulder, CO: Westview Press, 1989.
74. Alan Richards and John Waterbury, *A Political Economy of the Middle East: State, Class, and Economic Development*, Boulder, CO: Westview Press, 1990, pp. 436-7.
75. Ibid.
76. John Waterbury, 'The Soft State and the Open Door: Egypt's Experience with Economic Liberalization, 1974-1984,' *Comparative Politics*, 18(1), October 1985, 65-83.
77. Ibid.
78. Moench, 'The May 1984 Elections,' p. 70.
79. Ibid., p. 80.
80. *Al-Ahram* survey as cited by Robert Springborg in *Mubarak's Egypt*, p. 231.
81. Nicolas Gavrielides, 'Tribal Democracy: the Anatomy of Parliamentary Elections in Kuwait,' in Layne (ed.), *Elections in the Middle East*, p. 159.
82. Ibid., p. 176.
83. Ibid., p. 159.
84. Ibid.
85. Ibid.
86. Analysts have different takes on the import of irregularities and government interference in the elections. *The Economist*, for example, was critical in its 'Beduins Eatonsville,' February 1981, whereas Ahmad J. Daher and Faisal Al Salem praised the process in their 'Kuwait's Parliament Elections,' in the *Journal of Arab Studies*, 3(1) (1984), 85-98.
87. Kamal Osman Salih, 'Kuwait's Parliamentary Elections: 1963-1985: an Appraisal,' *Journal of South Asian and Middle Eastern Studies*, 16(2) (Winter 1992), 32.
88. Gavrielides, 'Tribal Democracy,' p. 181.
89. Ibid., p. 182.
90. Salih, 'Kuwait's Parliamentary Elections,' p. 32.
91. 'Tribal Voting Distribution,' *Al Qabbas*, January 26, 1985, 1, 6 [Joint Publications Research Service].
92. Ibid.
93. 'No Administrative Reform [without] Resolute, Just, and Equal Application of the Laws ...' an interview with Abd Al Aziz Al Saqr, *Al Mujtama*, April 2, 1985, 14-9 [Joint Publications Research Service].
94. Ibid., p. 14.

5. Foreign aid and reform: the diverging paths of Egypt and Jordan in the 1990s

Scholars have long recognized the potentially negative impact of foreign aid on the political and economic development of Third World states. Years ago, John Waterbury observed that infusions of external capital – especially of US foreign aid – had enabled the Egyptian government to forestall critical economic reforms in the late 1970s and early 1980s.[1] Subsequently, scholars of the 'rentier state' argued that exogenous revenues such as foreign aid insulated Middle Eastern rulers from political opposition, enabling them to avert political liberalization and democratization.[2]

In the late 1980s and 1990s, tremendous shifts in the provision of foreign aid to selected Middle Eastern countries have had dramatic effects on political life. In Jordan, the collapse of foreign aid revenues prompted the monarchy to initiate an unprecedented political liberalization. Meanwhile, in Egypt an extraordinary increase in foreign aid receipts encouraged the Mubarak regime to crack down on much of the opposition and to scale back political liberalization. Here, in comparing these cases, this chapter underscores the obligation of donors (who are largely interested in securing such geopolitical goals as Arab–Israeli peace and preventing the rise of Islamists) to consider the effects of foreign aid on democratic development. I seek to extend the conceptualizations of the rentier state literature by arguing that foreign aid flows may well have a critical impact on parliamentary life. In concrete terms, such flows have contributed to the emergence in Jordan – and to the demise in Egypt – of a substantial opposition. In recent years, Jordan has moved toward, and Egypt has moved from, the establishment of a meaningful multipartism. Given this important contrast, the focus of this chapter differs from that of the rest of this book. Instead of focusing on the impact of external capital on Middle Eastern development models, this chapter examines how such resources can shape – or undermine – political liberalization in the region. Here the comparison of Egypt and Jordan underscores the sweeping impact of exogenous resources on political and economic reform.

In the late 1980s and early 1990s, Jordan and Egypt approached economic reform, and their relations with international donors and financial institutions, from dramatically different perspectives. Each state sought to avoid far-reaching economic reforms for most of the 1970s and 1980s, relying on substantial exogenous revenues to avert economic crisis. In the 1980s, Egypt became the recipient of massive US aid contributions because of the Camp David Accords, which have further allowed it to insulate itself from economic and political reforms. But Jordan was not a beneficiary of this agreement, and with oil prices and aid flows declining by the late 1980s, most of Jordan's exogenous resources had evaporated. In turn, the Jordanian state experienced a crippling fiscal crisis that compelled the monarchy to reach a sweeping accommodation with the international financial institutions (IFIs). Equally important, the economic crisis and the watershed agreement with the IFIs precipitated a powerful political crisis. The government responded by extending significant political liberties and establishing a meaningful parliamentary process.

By contrast, in the late 1980s and early 1990s, Egypt had much greater exogenous resources, and therefore averted the political and economic crises that rocked Jordan. In receiving extraordinary amounts of foreign aid, the Mubarak regime had little incentive to engage in a risky political liberalization, or to offer its population increased political liberties in exchange for its acceptance of economic austerity. Indeed, from a relatively secure position, the regime engineered the demise of the significant parliamentary opposition that had existed in the 1980s.

The contrast between current Egyptian and Jordanian approaches to political reform is especially interesting in that each country has been grappling with painful economic reforms. Economic crisis has prompted Jordan to implement far-reaching political reforms. Meanwhile, exogenous windfalls have papered over Egypt's economic problems and have left the Mubarak regime free to repress its opposition during a disruptive period of economic austerity.

JORDAN: FROM ECONOMIC CRISIS TO POLITICAL REFORM

The search for foreign aid has long been a defining feature of Jordan's foreign policy and international relations. For most of its existence, the Jordanian state has been heavily reliant on grant-in-aid, bank loans, and other forms of external budgetary assistance. Until the late 1980s, rather than push for the expansion of a resource-poor domestic economy, the monarchy used its strategic position in the Arab–Israeli conflict to garner external revenues. Therefore, observes Laurie Brand, the state 'gradually evolved as primarily a distributor or an allocator [of the rents collected from outside] rather than an extractor of resources from within.' In this sense, the state enjoyed a 'relative autonomy from the input of societal forces.'³ The monarchy was able to maintain a highly repressive rule, so long as it provided the citizenry with a relatively high standard of living through the distribution of external rent.

Accordingly, before the electoral opening of 1989, parliamentary politics had never developed in any significant sense in Jordan. By and large, when operative, the parliament was a rubber-stamp institution. It had little influence on state policy – and certainly did not function as a meaningful forum for debate, dissent, and political expression. In 1957, the regime banned political parties, leaving popular and professional interests with few avenues for political participation. The parliament was suspended in 1974, and was replaced in 1977 by an even more ineffectual National Consultative Council, whose members were appointed by the king. In 1984, the regime reconvened the parliament. But by 1985, political repression increased again, and elections slated for 1986 were indefinitely postponed. A government crackdown on remaining pockets of political pluralism, especially among the Palestinians, continued into 1988. But recasting the Jordanian political landscape in 1988-9 was an economic crisis triggered by a steep decline in foreign aid from Arab Gulf sources. The result was – and clearly remains – one of the Arab world's most promising and far-reaching political openings, despite some setbacks that occurred in the late 1990s.

Through the 1970s and the early 1980s, Jordan had received roughly half its revenues in the form of foreign aid grants and loans. Such aid – mainly from the Gulf monarchies, but also from Western allies – was unquestionably the state's most important revenue source. For most of the 1970s and 1980s it enabled the state to maintain high levels of growth, expenditure, and consumption. But by 1988, the Jordanian economy slipped into a severe crisis, as the state's foreign aid receipts fell to roughly one-third of their 1980-1 level.⁴ By 1989, external capital accounted for only about one-quarter of government revenues.⁵ The state in turn was forced to reach an accommodation with the IMF and its international creditors, and to impose a relatively severe orthodox stabilization program in 1988 and 1989.

This sudden shift toward highly austere macroeconomic policies triggered a political crisis. In the words of Brand, 'the budget could no longer bear the regime's part of the political acquiescence bargain.'⁶ As the government's distributional capabilities declined, the population asserted itself. Severe civil disturbances rocked the country in April 1989, as thousands of Jordanians took to the streets. After quashing the protests, the regime took the risky strategic decision to engage in unprecedented political reform. It provided limited political liberties, released and pardoned political prisoners, and, above all, held parliamentary elections in November of 1989.

In those elections, the most significant since 1956, 877475 voters registered and 647 candidates competed, even though parties were still banned. The polling was free in most respects.[7] Indeed, Islamist candidates won a stunning victory, becoming strident opponents of the regime. The Muslim Brotherhood captured 22 of the parliament's 80 seats – the most of any faction – and allied with ten independent Islamists to form an Islamic bloc. Leftists and Arab and Palestinian nationalists won 11 seats, and pro-government candidates won 35 seats. Consequently, with the 1989 elections, parliamentary opposition emerged as a powerful force in Jordanian politics. As well, the 1989 polling initiated sweeping new political reforms. In 1990, the regime abolished anti-communist legislation, freed political prisoners, repealed martial law and allowed parties to function. By September of 1991, the authorities had officially approved roughly 90 parties.[8]

With the conduct of multiparty elections in 1993, the country's parliament had emerged as one of the region's most important democratic institutions. Some 1.2 million voters registered, and 536 candidates and 20 parties participated. A 4.7 percent increase in the number of voters seemed to reflect increased trust in the regime's democratization efforts. A change to a one-person, one-vote system did serve to reduce the number of Islamist parliamentarians, and to increase the number of independent or pro-regime ones.[9] But despite the protests of some activists, the 1993 polling was on the whole considered an important step in Jordanian democratization. In sum, the body had been endowed with genuine policy-making powers, had had consecutive open and free elections, and had come to express a vibrant multipartism.

Meanwhile, despite the revival of parliamentaly life, the regime did not relent in its implementation of economic orthodoxy. In the early 1990s, Jordan's receipt of exogenous revenues remained at low levels, and the regime had no choice but to adhere to macroeconomic austerity (see Table 5.1). Indeed, the structure of Jordanian state revenues experienced a transformation in the 1980s and 1990s. Its domestic revenues rose from 46 percent of total revenues in 1980[10] to 86 percent in 1993. In short, in response to the collapse of Arab aid, Jordan increased its revenues from direct and indirect taxation, with receipts from income and profits tax more than doubling in 1990, and

Table 5.1   The Jordanian central government budget of the 1990s: external vs. internal revenues (%)

	1990	1991	1992	1993
Domestic	79	75	86	86
Foreign	21	25	14	14

Source: Monthly Statistical Bulletin of the Central Bank of Jordan, as cited in Economist Intelligence Unit, *Jordan Country Profile, 1994–95,* London: The Economist, 1995, p. 28

with an overall increase in tax revenue of 59 percent in 1992.[11] As the Finance Minister Hanna Odeh noted, the regime was attempting to shift Jordan from a 'consuming to a producing society' that would be less vulnerable to vagaries in foreign exchange.[12]

After persuading East Bank loyalists that the economic reforms were unavoidable, the regime successfully defended its development program in the 1989 and 1993 elections. Its drawing of electoral districts – which discriminated against the urban vote and helped regime loyalists from rural areas – worked to prevent Islamists opposing the regime's new economic orthodoxy from obtaining an absolute parliamentary majority in 1989.[13] In the 1993 elections, the regime's electoral manipulations improved the standing of pro-orthodox loyalists, enabling them to ally with other forces to marshall a conservative parliamentary majority. As in other democratizing Third World states, such manipulations represented a successful attempt on the part of the regime to reconcile the exigencies of political and economic reform.[14]

In sum, the 'Jordanian glasnost,'[15] as the former foreign minister Taha Masri termed it, expressed the regime's interest in obtaining an electoral legitimation of its new development policies. It resembled the reform process in rent-poor Morocco, in that the coincidence of political and economic crises generated a substantive process of political liberalization.[16] In a word, powerful crises compelled the regime to seek a far-reaching electoral legitimation. Later in the chapter, I shall consider some setbacks to Jordanian political liberalization that occurred in the late 1990s. But on the whole, after the end of the decade, Jordan remains a leading political reformer in the region – in sharp contrast to Egypt.

THE MUBARAK REGIME OF THE 1990s: LIMITED ECONOMIC REFORMS, INCREASED REPRESSION AND A NEW DELUGE OF EXOGENOUS REVENUES

The maintenance of social welfare provisions was a critical concern of the Mubarak regime for most of the 1980s. Following the instability of 1979–81, which culminated in the assassination of President Anwar Sadat, Mubarak sought to reconsolidate the regime's control over the Egyptian polity. At the same time, Egypt was experiencing rapid economic growth – about 8 percent a year in the late 1970s and 1980s – which was fueled almost entirely by oil and foreign aid rents.[17] These seemingly favorable economic conditions enabled the insecure Mubarak regime to legitimate its rule by increasing its populist and statist expenditures. The regime postponed the economic reforms recommended by Western donors and creditors, portraying itself as a populist defender of the Egyptian masses.[18] In parliamentary openings in 1984 and

1987, the regime underscored its populist positioning. It ensured that its National Democratic Party (NDP) won majorities opposed by oppositions espousing right-wing and neoliberal economic policies. As well, the regime prevented left-wing parties (in other words, those to the left of the NDP) from gaining any meaningful representation in parliament.[19]

In the late 1980s, mounting debt and the collapse of oil prices caused a precipitous decline in Egyptian growth rates. As the 1990 parliamentary elections approached, the regime realized that it had to scale back its populist expenditures and adopt a more serious neoliberal reform program. But unlike other Arab states – for example, Morocco in 1983 and Jordan in 1988 – Egypt did not experience a foreign exchange crisis that left it in a weak bargaining position with the IFIs. Indeed, regional geopolitics enabled Egypt to obtain a uniquely generous accommodation with its donors: the Iraqi invasion of Kuwait, and the security interests of Western and Arab Gulf states, served to ease Egypt's cash flow problems. At the same time, Western and Gulf aid eviscerated the Mubarak regime's interest in political reform. For much of the 1980s exogenous revenues (in the form of foreign aid, loans, oil revenues, and Suez Canal tolls) accounted for between 40 percent and 50 percent of Egyptian state budget revenues.[20] The state slowly moved to reform the economy in the late 1980s, as its debts mounted and its oil revenues declined. But by 1990, the Egyptian economy was not in any sense in the throes of a crisis. Egyptian GDP in fact grew at an annual rate of 4.7 percent between 1986 and 1992.[21]

In the fall of 1990, as the US solicited Egyptian participation in the anti-Iraq coalition, the Egyptian government engaged in intense negotiations with its international donors and creditors. Ultimately, Egyptian officials agreed to implement substantial (though limited in key respects, as I argue below) economic reforms in exchange for an unprecedented exogenous windfall. Foreign aid to Egypt tripled during the three years following the Persian Gulf War. Between 1980 and 1989, Egypt annually received between $1.29 billion and $1.79 billion; during 1990–2, it garnered roughly $5 billion per year.[22] Additional concessions from Western donors and creditors, including massive debt relief, also dramatically increased the state's resources. After the Gulf War, for example, the United States and Arab governments agreed to cancel $13 billion worth of military debt. Soon thereafter, the Paris Club of creditor nations promised the eventual cancellation of $10 billion worth of loans in exchange for Egyptian promises of economic reform. Egypt, in short, had become the world's largest foreign aid recipient, claiming more than 10 percent of the $45 billion in overseas assistance distributed among over 150 countries.[23]

In appealing for aid during 1990, Egyptian officials argued that the Iraqi invasion of Kuwait might create a potentially destabilizing economic crisis in

Egypt: that the Gulf crisis had perhaps cost Egypt as much as $9 billion. Huge losses of revenues were expected to result from the mass expulsion of expatriate workers from Iraq and, to a lesser extent, from the decline in tourism and Suez Canal traffic. Drops in such revenues were in fact considerably less precipitous. The decline of expatriate remittances from the Gulf created a $1 billion drop in the balance of payments during 1990; the impact of the disruption of tourism and the Suez Canal traffic was considerably less substantial. These latter two revenue sources returned to healthy levels in 1991.[24] Meanwhile, massive aid, loans and debt relief from the international community vastly outstripped the decline in state revenues from remittances. Consequently, despite the serious losses resulting from the war, Egypt's exogenous resources increased dramatically in the 1990s.

The United States, Arab donors and international creditors and bankers have closely coordinated their aid efforts to achieve three aims: first, the foreign assistance has been a reward for Egyptian participation in the Gulf War; second, Western (and Arab) donors have used massive assistance to buy Egypt's implementation of limited economic reform; third, the donors have been concerned with the regime's political stability, and the threat from militant Islamists in particular. In attempting to finance Egypt's economic revival, in confronting its enduring poverty and economic inefficiency, the donors have sought to ensure the security of a regime that serves as the cornerstone of a pro-West regional stability.[25] Their concerns, notably, have not included substantial efforts to promote political liberalization or democratization.

FOREIGN AID: OBVIATING POLITICAL-ECONOMIC CRISIS

Massive foreign aid infusions have prevented in Egypt the cycle of economic crisis and political liberalization that occurred in Jordan. In 1990, because of the regional geopolitical crisis, Egypt was in a relatively strong position *vis-à-vis* its donors and creditors. It eventually extracted unprecedented levels of aid from the international financial community – and on comparatively lax terms that have softened economic austerity. The key point is that Jordan liberalized economically, largely because it lacked exogenous revenue. Extreme fiscal pressures created a political crisis that the regime sought to defuse through political liberalization.

By contrast, Egypt was not brought into a substantive reform process through a destabilizing political-economic crisis. Rather, the Mubarak regime agreed to limited economic liberalization to obtain extraordinary levels of exogenous resources. Such resources, from the regime's perspective, would in fact obviate the occurrence of the political-economic crisis that rocked states such as Jordan and Morocco. Like Guillermo O'Donnell and Philipe Schmitter, and others theorizing about the causes of political openings, I assume that a regime liberalizes politically and democratizes in order to deal with some manner of political or economic crisis.[26] Of course, crises do not necessarily prompt an authoritarian regime to liberalize. Yet during the last two decades a far-reaching crisis – and a state fiscal crisis in particular – has provided the most propitious context for the initiation of political liberalization. Indeed, in such Middle Eastern countries as Morocco and Jordan, the evaporation of exogenous resources have pushed regimes to implemented orthodox economic reform programs and to initiate significant political reforms. (A similar process occurred in Tunisia, though the regime's political reforms were short-lived.) Why did political liberalization increase in rent-poor Middle Eastern countries compelled to reach far-reaching agreements with the IFIs, but decline as the relatively rent-rich Egypt implemented its version of neoliberal economic reforms? The Egyptian case demonstrates the ability of foreign aid flows to shape – or disrupt – Third World political development. For the Mubarak regime, *before* the advent of economic crisis, apparently calculated that the acquisition of massive aid would alleviate political pressures on the regime and obviate the need to cope with issues of economic reform through a defining political opening.

Above all, unlike other Middle Eastern regimes, the Mubarak regime moved toward economic orthodoxy while its control over the political system was relatively secure. Indeed, during 1990 and 1991, as Egypt drew closer to the international financial community and began to accept the new foreign assistance, the Mubarak regime was, in the words of one observer, 'without any serious challenger.' The secular opposition remained badly fragmented; and the power of the Islamists, particularly of the Muslim Brotherhood, had also waned, largely because of dissaray in the Islamic investment houses. As well, during and after the Gulf War, the regime enjoyed broad popular support for its handling of the crisis and its stance against Iraq (which for years had mistreated the two million Egyptian expatriate workers there).[27] In turn, the aid enhanced its position, halting the movement toward increased political liberalization which had been prominent during the 1980s.

In fact, a limited closing of the political-electoral system took place in 1990. In deference to supreme court rulings that the parliamentary electoral laws were illegal, Mubarak dissolved the People's Assembly which had been elected in 1987. But in drafting new electoral codes, the regime designed a single-member electoral system that disadvantaged the interests of the major opposition forces: most importantly, the Wafd and the Moslem Brotherhood. Most of the opposition boycotted the elections, and the NDP ultimately obtained 91 percent of the seats. Consequently, in creating an electoral system that was obviously unacceptable to the major opposition forces, the regime effectively constricted the political liberalization process. The coincidence of the narrowing of political space and the deluge of foreign aid illustrates the rentier state thesis: namely, high levels of exogenous revenues may well militate against processes of political liberalization and democratization. In the end, a rentier windfall worked to constrict the Egyptian polity, whereas resource gaps served to liberalize other Middle Eastern states.

FOREIGN AID AND VITAL ELECTORAL FACTIONS

Stagnation was the key feature of Egyptian politics during the 1990s. Under Mubarak, the NDP has retained its institutional structure, minor cabinet shuffles and shifts in the regime's attitudes toward reform notwithstanding. Unlike Jordan and Morocco, Egypt has not experienced the emergence of vigorous parliamentary competition; nor has the NDP attempted to reform or reorganize itself in any substantive way. The regime made provisions for the political participation of center-right forces in the 1980s, but did so within the context of the opposition, and through the Wafd and the Muslim Brotherhood in particular. The regime's indulgence of the Egyptian opposition in the 1984 and 1987 parliaments dissipated in the early 1990s. With one opposition party, the leftist Tagamu, winning but six seats in 1991, the parliament no longer functioned as a locus of meaningful competitive party politics.

The regime seemed to reach an important milestone in 1994 with its renewed repression of the Muslim Brotherhood. By June, most Brotherhood leaders were in jail on charges of incitement or complicity in terrorism. The government seemed to be returning the organization to an illegitimate status, branding it 'terrorist' for the first time since Mubarak reopened the political system in the early 1980s. Said Issam al-Irian, a senior Brotherhood leader:

> This is the first time the government has linked us to terrorism. It is a wide move by the government to curtail all forms of democracy ... by narrowing the opportunities for democratic participation, the government is creating more problems than it is solving.

Another Brotherhood activist noted that the repression would make the movement more extremist, as members who had moderated their political positions to participate in the parliament in the 1980s became increasingly disillusioned. 'What do you expect?' he asked.[28]

As well, secular opposition members who had advocated parliamentary participation in the 1980s have become increasingly alienated during the 1990s. One prominent member of the Wafd's 'old guard,' for example, has maintained that the current parliament is nothing but 'a branch of the dominant party.' He has observed that the party's participation in elections under the current regime is probably 'pointless.'[29] That Wafdists have such opinions is predictable enough, given the demise of oppositional politics in the parliament of the 1990s. It is also a far cry from their optimism of the mid-1980s, when party leaders predicted, if only for propagandistic purposes, that the New Wafd would eventually come to dominate the parliament and the polity.[30]

Surely, independent and NDP members of the parliament have been considerably more sanguine about the body's prospects. They, of course, still presume that parliamentary life signifies a true process of 'democratization.'[31] Consequently, some members seem to believe that the parliament eventually will become increasingly representative, inclusive, and vociferous in the near future. One highly regarded independent has argued that pressure from the US and from a young generation of educated, restless, CNN-watching Egyptians ultimately will push the regime to expand the parliamentary process. Like other members of the Egyptian political elite, she believes that the United States is responsible for, and will promote, democracy in Egypt. On her view, economic dependence on the US and other Western nations, and the consequent 'liberalization' of the country's economic system, will prompt increasingly autonomous social forces to push for democratization.[32]

Naturally, Egyptian dissidents have had a more realistic estimation of the impact of foreign aid on political life. On their view, genuine Egyptian democratic activity has withered. Though not necessarily opposing Egypt's receipt of massive foreign aid, prominent human rights activists are particularly sensitive to the fact that such aid increases the ability of the regime to stifle movement towards democracy.[33] Their gloomy predictions of political stagnation seem sound for the foreseeable future, given the Mubarak regime's apparent reluctance to liberalize politically during a difficult period of economic adjustment.

Considering the West's poor record of promoting democracy in the Arab world, the insiders' and independents' claim that external forces will push Egypt to democratize in the near term seems fatuous. As well, the regime's inability or unwillingness to undertake restructuring projects like privatization seems to ensure that powerful social forces clamoring for more democracy will not be unleashed anytime soon. Indeed, the last half of the 1990s was a catastrophe for Egyptians hoping for increased political liberties.

THE 1995 ELECTIONS: CHAOS AND THUGGERY

The parliamentary elections of November and December 1995 only reconfirmed the regime's lack of interest in establishing any significant multipartism. The regime seemed to begin its pre-election crackdown during the preceding January, as it renewed its harassment of the Brotherhood. On November 23, 54 Islamist professionals, including parliamentary candidates, were sentenced by a military court to three to five years in prison. The regime then closed the Brotherhood's Cairo headquarters and arrested dozens of activists. The interior minister, Hassan Alfi, asserted that the Brotherhood – the most important opposition group, and one that officially denounces violence – was a greater threat to security than the Islamist radicals who have waged a bloody campaign against the state for the past three years.[34]

Such ominous developments gave way to the bloodiest elections in the history of modern Egypt: 40 people were killed and between 400 and 700 were injured in polling dominated by fraud, vote-buying, chaos, intimidation, and sectarian violence. On December 7, the NDP won 317 seats, independents won 113 and opposition parties won 14. But the next day, 99 independents *re*joined the NDP, giving it 416, or 94 percent, of the seats. Denouncing the results, the opposition called for new elections and the dissolution of the body.

In short, parliamentary politics have become increasingly irrelevant in Egypt. After the 1995 ballot, the Egyptian Human Rights Legal Aid Center warned of a 'political explosion because the chances of peaceful change seem to be non-existent.'[35] In subsequent years, the government has effectively repressed leading opposition groups, particularly Islamist ones, thereby avoiding (thus far) any political explosions. But in the latter half of the 1990s, Egyptian political liberalization continued to contract. The parliament, lacking any serious opposition, had in fact become a rather pathetic political club for the NDP.

Following his election to a fourth six-year presidential term in October 1999 – after winning 94 percent of the vote in a 'presidential referendum' – Mubarak acknowledged the problematic parliamentary stagnation. He floated the idea of organizing leading businessmen within a new party (called the Future). Egyptians simply understood him to mean that Mubarak's version of political reform would continue to be highly incremental and perhaps barely noticeable. Appropriately, 1999 also featured a renewed repression of the Brotherhood.

During the 1990s, exogenous revenues have reinforced these political directions. Throughout these years, the Egyptian state retained its access to extraordinary exogenous resources. Indeed, by 1995 it had amassed $17 billion in foreign exchange reserves, which made the regime, observers noted, immune to pressures from the IFIs to reform the economy.[36] IMF complaints for much of the decade included an inflated exchange rate, high inflation, spiraling public-sector wages, high industrial subsidies, and an almost complete lack of movement on privatization, trade liberalization, and civil service reforms.[37]

In a report for the 1995 Amman economic summit, the IMF expressed its displeasure with the sluggishness of Egyptian economic reforms, and applauded Jordan (along with Tunisia and Morocco) for being one of the leading economic reformers in the Arab world.[38] Current IMF attitudes toward the two countries underscored the divergence of the Jordanian and Egyptian paths. Since 1988, in lacking nonconditional funding, Jordan has not had much leeway in its dealings with the IFIs. As well, in becoming increasingly reliant on domestic revenue sources (that is, taxation), King Husayn had no choice but to acquiesce in popular demands for democratization. Here parliament has become a useful venue for a wide-ranging debate about the scope and meaning of economic reforms. By contrast, in Egypt, exogenous windfalls have given the regime greater freedom of action in its dealings with the IFIs. Nonconditional funding also has augmented the regime's political latitude, forestalling any manner of parliamentary accommodation with the opposition forces that have been calling for increased democratization for the last 20 years.

More recently, Jordan has not been a paragon of democratic development, though it has remained a leading example of political liberalization in the Arab world. Stung by vitriolic criticisms of his rapprochement with Israel, and in the wake of the assassination of Israeli Prime Minister Yitzhak Rabin, King Husayn formulated stricter laws governing freedoms of associations and the press in December 1995. In June 1997, the government passed laws clearly meant to restrict the press, as well as stifle academic and other expressions of debate and free speech. A further setback came in 1997, as leading opposition groups boycotted parliamentary elections to protest against restrictive electoral laws implemented by the government.

But overall, even given these reversals, Jordanian political liberalization has achieved – or at any rate maintained – some critical achievements during the latter half of the 1990s. Through 1999, the Jordanian parliament remained an important locus of oppositional activity, in spite of the botched elections of 1997. Roughly one-third of parliamentary seats are still held by individuals opposing government policies. Perhaps most important, in controlling at times as much as one-third of parliament during the 1990s, Islamists have been able to rally opposition to the king's policies. Since 1989, parliamentary opposition has often had a critical impact on government policy. Furthermore, the parliament has remained a meaningful mechanism of popular political participation and expression, even as the government has had its way with the institution. For example, though the parliament ultimately ratified the austere 1996 budget, debate over the government's economic policies, and its handling of poverty and unemployment, was heated.[39] This is evidence of a dynamically developing system.

In recent months the parliament has worked to expose government scandals and curb the regime's arbitrary use of power. Further, in 1999 municipal elections, the leading opposition group – the Muslim Brotherhood and its political wing, the Islamic Action Front (IAF) – realized stunning victories in five major cities: of its 100 candidates, 72 won city council seats. Building on these successes, the Brotherhood and the IAF have indicated their interest in competing in the 2001 parliamentary elections and in deepening their involvement in the nascent Jordanian electoral process.

Meanwhile, Egyptian parliamentary life has stagnated in the 1990s. Being supported by unprecedented levels of exogenous revenue, and having a gradualist and inconsistent approach to economic development, the regime has refrained from developing any kind of vital electoral factions. During the 1990s, as foreign aid obviated the need to impose a sweeping austerity, the NDP has not attempted to use parliament as a serious venue for political discussion and participation. Attempting to incorporate the major viewpoints of both the right and the left during the 1990s, the NDP has been content with its domination of a lilliputian parliamentary opposition. In Jordan, the evaporation of foreign aid rents ultimately led to a clearer definition of political possibilities, which were vigorously discussed in the parliament.

Here the fiscal crisis compelled the Jordanian regime to tolerate – and to develop – increasingly sophisticated electoral coalitions. Having ensured the dominance of a coalition calling for an unpopular austerity, the regime also was obliged to tolerate the activities of opposition groups. Even so, and until the government decides to directly attack the parliamentary process that it has allowed to grow in Jordan, it remains a leading example of political liberalization in the Arab world. Therefore, Jordanian liberalization and Egyptian repression remain stark contrasts, especially as Jordan has continued to develop its electoral process through 1999 and into 2000, under the rule of the new king Abdullah II.

MULTIPARTISM AND POLITICAL LIBERALIZATION AMID ECONOMIC AUSTERITY: THE IMPORTANCE OF CONDITIONALITY?

Multipartism represents the substantive and (for the regime) risky dimension of political openings. In the Middle Eastern context of liberalizing authoritarianism, it suggests a substantive parliamentary accommodation with opposition forces. Ideally, multipartism implies some kind of power-sharing, by curbing the power of the ruling party and enabling opponents to participate in some aspect of the policy-making process. Presumably, this process has the potential to evolve some day into a genuine democratization. Moreover, in the short-term, multipartism enables opposition groups to protect newly extended political liberties, including freedoms of movement, speech, petition, dissent and so forth. As such, the regime sanctions and institutionalizes a delimitation of its power. Substantive multipartism emerges, because the regime believes that it signifies the best strategy for the forging of some kind of 'democratic bargain' with a citizenry suffering the effects of economic crisis and austerity. Its development in Jordan has followed the evaporation of its exogenous resources, the onset of economic crisis and the regime's acceptance of far-reaching neoliberal reforms. Of course, such a crisis does not guarantee, but merely provides a favorable context for, the regime's implementation of serious political liberalization.

Typically, the nature of the crisis dictates the extent to which regime elites are willing to permit liberalization and democratization. A manageable crisis or challenge tends to translate into a highly limited or controlled liberalization. Intense pressure – a near collapse of a key revenue flow, for example – limits the ability of the regime elites to control the political opening, and gives more leverage to an opposition seeking genuine democratization. Similarly, Patrick Clawson has argued that difficult economic circumstances have enhanced the prospects for democratization in the Middle East.[40] But the disintegration of external sources of support seems to create a particularly compelling crisis, as state elites must extract more internal revenues and reach a more substantial parliamentary accommodation with leading opposition groups. Conversely, this line of analysis underscores the negative aspects of massive aid to authoritarian rulers.

Of course, Western aid to the Middle East is not oriented toward democratic development, but toward the promotion of geopolitical stability and Arab-Israeli peace. It is not primarily a matter of democratic development projects, such as those of the US Agency for International Development (USAID), being small, underfunded or ineffective. Rather, in countries like Egypt, massive foreign aid has been used primarily to preserve decades-old statist and authoritarian structures. At the same time, donors have considered aid to Egypt and other Arab countries to be a critical support of the peace process and the maintenance of a pro-Western geopolitical order. Since such aid decreases reformist pressures on the regime, the promotion of peace and the promotion of democracy seem to contradict one another, as Lisa Anderson has observed. This conclusion, she notes:

> presents genuine and important dilemmas for policy makers, faced with hopes not only for peace and democracy but also for a stable, pacific and democratic world that is inexpensive to create and maintain.[41]

By definition, such dilemmas defy facile solutions. But this chapter suggests a basic incoherence in Western policies toward the issues of economic and political reform in the Middle East. That incoherence flows from the nature of the conditionality imposed upon the foreign aid to Arab states.

Notwithstanding the official lip service paid to the promotion of democracy in the Arab Middle East, the array of Western aid to the region is intended, above all, to foster a friendly geopolitical environment and the implementation of neoliberal economic reforms. Through conditionality, the IFIs have forced governments in the Middle East to take basic steps toward economic reform. Indeed, conditionality has been the driving force behind the adoption of neoliberal reforms in the developing world.[42] Western donors have not flinched from using the provision of foreign aid to impose harsh economic austerity and restructuring. But, fearing political instability, they have refrained from demanding serious political reforms from their Middle Eastern clients. Indeed, the foreign aid projects have often only delayed such political reforms.

If Western donors are serious about promoting democracy in the region, they must consider linking foreign aid to the regimes' adoption of political reforms and the respect for basic political and civil freedoms. Ultimately, that conditionality should provide the regimes with the incentive to develop some form of meaningful multipartism. That prescription may sound radical to some practitioners. Yet the provision of US foreign aid sometimes has been premised on such concerns in other world areas. The State Department perhaps already has recognized the need for increased leverage in the case of its Egyptian client: in recent years it occasionally criticized the repression of the Brotherhood and the implosion of the Egyptian electoral process.

More generally, practitioners might object that such a conditionality defies the rules of *Realpolitik*. But humanitarianism aside, nonconditional support of decaying authoritarian regimes only undermines Western interests, as it radicalizes oppositions and precludes the possibilities for peaceful change.

NOTES

1. John Waterbury, 'The "Soft State" and the Open Door: Egypt's Experience with Economic Liberalization, 1974–1984,' *Comparative Politics*, 24 (1991), 68.
2. Hazem Beblawi and Giacomo Luciani (eds), *Nation, State and Integration in the Arab World: The Rentier State*, London: Croom Helm, 1987.
3. Laurie Brand, *Jordan's Inter-Arab Relations: The Political Economy of Alliance Making*, New York: Columbia University Press, 1994, p. 82.
4. See government revenue tables for Jordan, in Victor Lavy and Eliezer Sheffer, *Foreign Aid and Economic Development in the Middle East: Egypt, Syria and Jordan*, New York: Praeger, 1991; or Robert Satloff, 'Jordan's Great Gamble: Economic Crisis and Political Reform,' in Henri J. Barkey (ed.), *The Politics of Economic Reform in the Middle East*, New York: St Martin's Press, 1992, p. 131.
5. The Economist Intelligence Unit, *Country Report: Jordan, 1993*, London: The Economist.
6. Brand, *Jordan's Inter-Arab Relations*, p. 291.
7. Abla Amawi, 'Jordan,' in Frank Tachau (ed.), *Political Parties of the Middle East and North Africa*, Westport, CT: Greenwood Press, 1994, p. 266.
8. Ibid., p. 267.

9. Ibid., p. 269.
10. The Economist Intelligence Unit, *Jordan Country Profile, 1994-95*, London: The Economist, p. 28.
11. Ibid.
12. Satloff, 'Jordan's Great Gamble,' p. 136.
13. Ibid., p. 143.
14. See Robert Kaufman, 'Liberalization and Democratization in South America: Perspectives from the 1970s,' in Guillermo O'Donnell and Philippe Schmitter (eds), *Transitions from Authoritarian Rule: Comparative Perspectives*, Baltimore, MD: Johns Hopkins University Press, 1986.
15. Satloff, 'Jordan's Great Gamble,' p. 143.
16. See my discussion of Morocco in 'External Capital and Political Liberalization: a Typology of Middle Eastern Development in the 1980s and 1990s,' *Journal of International Affairs*, 49(1) (1995), 70.
17. *The Economist*, April 7, 1984, 65.
18. See my discussion of Egypt in 'External Capital,' 64-8.
19. Richard Moench, 'The May 1984 Elections in Egypt and the Question of Egypt's Stability,' in Linda Layne (ed.), *Elections in the Middle East: Implications of Recent Trends*, Boulder, CO: Westview Press, 1987, p. 57.
20. See my discussion of Egypt in 'External Capital,' 53-64.
21. *The Middle East*, July/August 1995, 28.
22. William E. Schmidt, 'A Deluge of Foreign Assistance Fails to Revive Egypt's Stricken Economy,' *New York Times*, October 17, 1993, 10.
23. Ibid.
24. The Economist Intelligence Unit, *World Outlook, 1991*, London: The Economist, 1991, p. 102.
25. Schmidt, 'A Deluge of Foreign Assistance.'
26. Guillermo O'Donnell and Philippe Schmitter (eds), *Transitions from Authoritarian Rule: Tentative Conclusions about Uncertain Democracies*, Baltimore, MD: Johns Hopkins University Press, 1986, p. 16.
27. Economist Intelligence Unit, *World Outlook, 1991*, p. 102.
28. Quoted in Chris Hedges, 'Egypt Begins Crackdown on Strongest Opposition Group,' *New York Times*, June 12, 1984, 3.
29. Personal interview with Muhamed Asfur, February 1994.
30. Ibrahim Dessouki Abaza, 'Congratulations, Wafd,' *Al Wafd* (in Arabic), June 7, 1984, 3.
31. Conversation with Muhamed Al Tuwab Al Mohandis (former NDP member of parliament), February 1994.
32. Personal interview with Mona Makram Ebeid, February 1994.
33. Conversations with Dr Muhamed Mandour, Sabir Ahmed Mahmud Nayal (head of the Cairo division of Amnesty International), and Abdel Rahman Al Zein (Amnesty activist), December 1993 and January 1994.
34. 'Vote or Fight,' *The Economist*, December 2, 1995, 38-9.
35. Quoted by the Arab Press Service, Diplomat News Service, December 18, 1995.
36. *Middle East Economic Digest*, June 2, 1995, 28.
37. *Middle East*, July/August 1995, 28.
38. *Middle East Economic Digest*, September 22, 1995.
39. Xinhua News Agency, January 4, 1996.
40. Patrick Clawson, 'What's So Good about Stability?' in Henri J. Barkey (ed.), *The Politics of Economic Reform in the Middle East*, New York: St Martin's Press, 1992.
41. Lisa Anderson, 'Peace and Democracy in the Middle East: the Constraints of Soft Budgets,' *Journal of International Affairs*, 49(1) (Summer 1995), 44.
42. Barbara Stallings, 'International Influence on Economic Policy: Debt, Stabilization, and Structural Reform,' in Stephan Haggard and Robert Kaufman (eds), *The Politics of Economic Adjustment*, Princeton, NJ: Princeton University Press, 1992.

6. Distinctive development trajectories in the Middle East

This study has focused on the distinctive electoral designs and development strategies of four Middle Eastern countries in an era of neoliberal economic reform. In the 1960s and 1970s, Turkey, Morocco, Egypt, and Kuwait all pursued expansive state-led development strategies. In the 1970s, as their economies faced mounting difficulties, the Turkish, Moroccan, and Egyptian governments implemented mild reforms. But those efforts remained quite limited and indeed superficial; for these states retained access to copious amounts of 'nonconditional' finance, which papered over structural inefficiencies in their economies.

The dynamics of Third World development changed dramatically in the 1980s, with the onset of a global recession and the tightening of international credit. Countries throughout the developing world confronted debt and foreign exchange crises. In exchange for emergency finance, the IFIs demanded that Third World countries implement stabilization and structural adjustment. Such 'conditionality' ensured that countries forced into official agreements with the IFIs undertook some manner of serious economic reform.[1]

This study has focused on the ability of four Middle Eastern states to cope with pivotal crises, be they economic or political. I consider their regimes' development programs and parliamentary designs to be the results or legacies of specific crises. That is, in facing crises, they create political and economic orders that balance and reconcile their abilities to manufacture legitimacy and accumulate revenue. I am not arguing, at the same time, that exogenous rent levels fix those orders and determine all important facets of electoral life. Of course, central political and economic structures evolve continually, even as exogenous rent levels remain fairly constant. Nevertheless, during defining crises, exogenous rent levels encourage a regime to establish a distinctive and enduring set of legacies and policies.

This study has argued that state access to external capital is a critical factor in the development of electoral processes and political openings. Heretofore, the democratic transitions literature has emphasized that strategic interactions among political elites condition political liberalization and democratization. Accordingly, this literature has maintained that electoral and constitutional designs – for example, whether the new regime is presidential or parliamentary – may have critical implications for democratic development. It has also underscored the importance of the culture and attitudes of the political elite in the shaping of electoral openings. Here analysts have sought to counsel politicians, praising the democratic virtues of conciliation and compromise.[2]

With this study, I have not sought to argue against the relevance of institutional arrangements and elite attitudes. Still, one must understand how such arrangements and attitudes are situated within the larger structures of the international economy and the state's system of revenue accumulation. In focusing on the decisive impact of exogenous revenues in electoral openings, this study suggests limits to the elite-based approaches.

Here, I summarize the important trends in political and economic development of the four cases in the 1980s and early 1990s, and consider other important electoral openings in the region in these years. I also reflect on the importance of exogenous revenues on economic reform in countries throughout the Middle East. My aim is to demonstrate that my hypotheses describe a predominant regional development process in the 1980s and 1990s.

I then reflect on the connection between economic and political reforms, and on the relationship between parliamentary multipartism and political liberalization. I conclude by discussing the nonregional comparativist literature on the question of the sequencing of political and economic reforms.

My comparisons of the four cases have started with the Turkish case, which had the fewest exogenous resources and was the earliest and most substantive economic reformer in the region. I have argued that that country's severe political and economic crises of the late 1970s and early 1980s were inextricably intertwined. The outgoing military regime sought in the early 1980s to shift a crisis-prone inward-oriented economy toward export-led and austerity-based development, and to create a political system that would protect and legitimate this new socioeconomic order.

Many Turks, especially in the social democratic movement, were convinced that the military intervention, the subsequent redesign of the constitution and the electoral laws, the agreements with the international financial community, and ultimately the rise of the MP, had effectively ended the era of Turkish populism and import substitution. The new rules of the game, it seemed, would guarantee Turkish austerity and anti-populism for the indefinite future.[3]

As it turns out, MP administrations of the late 1980s continued to preach macroeconomic orthodoxy, but in fact eventually implemented some of the subsidies and inflationary policies that had served as central redistributive instruments in the postwar era. In this sense, argues Andrew Mango, the 'demise' of Turkish populism has been overstated.[4]

What, then, were the legacies of the Turkish crisis of the late 1970s and early 1980s? They included the reorganization of the political system on anti-populist lines; the augmentation of the power of the right in general; the unprecedented rise to political power of the export-oriented business sector in particular; and the implementation of economic programs that were, by Turkish and regional standards, highly austere, orthodox, and anti-populist.

These legacies have had a decisive impact on the Turkish political economy. In the short term (1980–4), the regime maintained draconian budgetary policies. In the medium term, it provided for the political dominance of pro-orthodox private sector groups; and it established a restrictive political order, one that was gradually relaxed in the late 1980s. In the long term, the regime created far and away the most sustained and far-reaching privatization, liberalization, and export promotion project in the Middle East. This new political economy, moreover, has been based on a long-term erosion of popular economic rights. Between 1980 and 1988, national income was redistributed *en masse* from the sectors of agriculture, wages, and salaries to those of profits, rents, and interest incomes. That is, during this period, farmers' income as a percentage of national income declined from 26.7 percent to 13.2 percent; wages and salaries dropped from 23.9 percent to 15.8 percent; and rents, profits, and income increased from 49.5 percent to 71 percent.[5]

In sum, the economic crisis of the late 1970s and early 1980s and the subsequent coup recast the trajectory of Turkish political development. Consequently, the new political economy remained predominant, even as the center-right True Path Party ultimately replaced the more orthodox Motherland Party as the dominant political force in the 1991 elections.

Like Turkey, Morocco faced a faltering economy, and a foreign exchange crisis in particular, in the early 1980s. The economic crisis, having commenced in the late 1970s, forced the regime to move toward an increasingly export-oriented and austerity-based model. As in Turkey, the economic crisis worked to destabilize the political system during these years. Like the Turkish junta in 1983, the Moroccan government in 1984 sought the legitimation of its neoliberal programs through parliamentary elections.

I identify three chief legacies from this period. One is, of course, the creation of one of the more austere, consistent, and far-reaching neoliberal models among major countries in the region. The Moroccan political economy of the 1980s, like the Turkish model, consistently eroded the income of the popular sectors and increased the wealth of bourgeois groups linked to international capital. For most of the 1980s and 1990s, the regime showed exceptional discipline in its budgetary policies: cutting expenditures, slashing deficits, maintaining low inflation, improving the current account, and so forth. Consequently, by the early 1990s, the international financial institutions considered Morocco a model debtor.

Second, because of the crisis, King Hassan sought the rationalization of the parliamentary organization and participation of a center-right bourgeoisie. That is, through the creation of the Constitutional Union, the regime attempted to modernize and formalize bourgeois interests that would champion the new economic programs.

The third legacy was the creation of more vital multipartist electoral factions in Morocco in the 1980s and 1990s. In the era of economic reform and austerity, the regime has reached unprecedented electoral accommodations with oppositional forces, first in 1984, and then to an even greater extent in 1993. Opposition parties, of course, existed in Morocco in the 1960s and 1970s. But they did not obtain any meaningful parliamentary representation until economic crisis forced the regime to permit a more substantial political liberalization in the 1980s and 1990s. As I argue below, in becoming a minimally rentier state in the late 1980s, Jordan followed a similar trajectory: economic crisis compelled the Jordanian regime to liberalize its political system. Since Morocco and Jordan have had the most far-reaching political openings of the major Arab states, one might consider that the evaporation of exogenous resources offers the best prospects for meaningful political liberalization in the Arab world.

Egypt's exogenous windfalls of the late 1970s and early 1980s pushed the Mubarak regime in rather different political-economic directions. The 1984 parliamentary elections in Egypt helped the Mubarak regime to define the boundaries of political and economic discourse in the post-Sadat era. Following the instability of the 1979–81 period, the crackdown on opposition groups and the assassination of President Anwar Sadat, the 1984 poll marked the revival of Egyptian political liberalization, and the reconsolidation of the regime's control over legitimate political life. Concomitantly, the regime relied on exogenous rents to postpone the economic reforms demanded by the international creditor community, and to increase popular consumption and the provision of services. While Turkey and Morocco embraced neoliberal orthodoxy in the early 1980s, Egyptian policies became increasingly heterodox. In the end, the Mubarak regime designed a political opening that highlighted the government's populist stance, and made the neoliberal bourgeoisie (through the Wafd) its parliamentary opposition.

During the late 1980s and early 1990s, the Egyptian regime developed increasingly intimate ties with the IMF and World Bank. But that movement toward increased orthodoxy was extremely sluggish throughout the 1980s; and the enduring government policies continued to focus on the preservation of the Egyptian social fabric and the protection of the interests of the popular sectors. The government maintained, above all, most of the welfare policies of the Nasirist era. By the end of the 1980s, in the minds of many scholars, the new Sphinx's riddle was the Egyptian reluctance to implement economic reform.[6]

Quite simply, for most of the 1980s, the Egyptian regime averted neo-liberalism, because its exogenous resources had yet to dissipate. As its rents declined in the latter half of the decade – due to the oil glut and its mounting debt burden – Egyptian economic reforms accelerated, especially in the early 1990s. Still, the Egyptian trajectory differs from that of the minimally rentier states in critical respects. First, the regime continues to rely on exogenous rents to forestall and mitigate the demands of international creditors: the regime has not catered to the interests of a center-right bourgeoisie, nor has it imposed austerity and anti-populism, to the extent that Morocco and Turkey have.[7] Second, and unlike the two minimally rentier states, Egypt has not sought to reorganize the political system in ways that enhance and streamline the parliamentary power of the center-right. Third, and most important, Egypt's implementation of orthodoxy in the early 1990s was undertaken *in exchange for* positively extraordinary exogenous windfalls (in the form of unprecedented levels of foreign aid from Western and Gulf donors). Consequently, Egypt's imposition of economic reform during the 1990s coincided not with an opening, but with a closing of the political system. In sum, the Egyptian regime's access to extraordinary exogenous revenues has conditioned its approach to political and economic reform, and has distinguished its development from that of the minimally rentier states.

Finally, the Kuwaiti parliamentary process of the 1980s accelerated anti-bourgeois political trends that had existed for decades. Since the advent of the National Assembly in 1963, the regime has used that body to weaken the political power of the highly cohesive Kuwaiti bourgeoisie. That class had been, after the royal family, the pre-eminent political power and had embodied the parliamentary movement during the pre-oil era. By the 1981–6 parliaments, and with the reinstatement of the National Assembly in 1991, the Kuwaiti bourgeoisie had been reduced to one of several Kuwaiti 'opposition' groups.

In 1981, to increase support among Kuwaiti nationals and to cope with threats created by the Iranian revolution and the Iran–Iraq War, the Al Sabah regime re-established the parliament in elections that reaffirmed the political marginalization of the bourgeoisie. That marginalization reflected the regime's need to cultivate allies who were more diverse and controllable than the business elite. In a word, the regime needed to broaden and popularize its alliances.

The parliament of the 1980s then endorsed the regime's highly expansionary budgets, which increased support for a range of social and sectarian groups. Here the regime was increasing subsidies (for such basic items as petrol and electricity) that the minimally rentier states were determined to eliminate or roll back, and that the Egyptian regime had indulged cautiously in the early 1980s.

Consequently, the Kuwaiti reinstatement of parliament was designed to enhance and legitimate policies that the electoral openings of the two minimally rentier states were intended to undermine. It sought not to scale back 'popular' rights, but to augment them; and it effected not the empowerment of bourgeois groups, but the decline of their political fortunes. In sum, the principal Kuwaiti legacy of the 1980s was the consolidation of pro-Beduin and anti-bourgeois trends. In the end, unlike the minimally and semi-rentier states, Kuwait has been able to marginalize the bourgeoisie's parliamentary role, since it does not need to incorporate this class into its development model.

SUBSEQUENT ELECTORAL DEVELOPMENTS IN THE FOUR CASES

In 1987, Turkey's anti-populist electoral codes, as designed by the junta, once again helped the Motherland Party to win the parliamentary elections and maintain itself as the dominant force in the government.[8] At the same time, in the late 1980s and early 1990s, popular pressures caused the relaxation of some of the authoritarian and exclusionary constraints that the military rulers had placed on political and economic life. Opposition groups forced the government to remove anti-democratic biases from the electoral codes. As well, in the late 1980s and early 1990s, MP administrations relaxed the austerity that had been imposed on the Turkish economy in the early and middle 1980s. This return to more populist and inflationary policies reflected two factors. It stemmed from, above all, an upsurge in the exogenous resources available to the Turkish state. Having won kudos for its economic reforms, the government was able to resume heavy borrowings on lax terms from international commercial sources. As Miles Kahler observes, this upsurge in the state's 'nonconditional' resources – this exogenous windfall – encouraged Turkish policy-makers to stray from economic orthodoxy in the late 1980s.[9] Here vagaries in Turkish macroeconomic policy reflected vagaries in the flows of exogenous revenues.

Second, the turn toward heterodox policies reflected the MP's need to cater to popular demands and consolidate its electoral position.[10] Thus, redemocratization prompted, as it did in Brazil, Argentina, and elsewhere, an increase in expansionary macroeconomic policies.[11] Haggard and Kaufman have shown that redemocratizing regimes are especially ineffective in implementing or maintaining neoliberal orthodoxy, and I have maintained that the effects of exogenous revenues are most clearly visible in relatively strong, stable and cohesive states. In this sense, the full Turkish redemocratization of the late 1980s has been beyond the parameters of typology, which has addressed the ability of strong and relatively insulated authoritarian regimes to implement economic and political reforms. All the while, the current Turkish political economy still reflects the neoliberal vision of the policy-makers of the early 1980s, in being based on the long-term erosion of popular rights, privatization, and export promotion.[12] The rise of the MP in 1983 was pivotal in this process.

By contrast, political and economic change in Morocco has reflected the regime's stable authoritarian rule. Among Arab countries, Morocco has been one of the leading economic reformers, and has implemented the most successful privatization program.[13] While consistently maintaining economic austerity in the 1980s and 1990s, the regime was able to postpone parliamentary elections until 1993 . That polling marked a significant opening of the political system, in that opposition parties were permitted unprecedented success – indeed a victory – in the direct elections. Equally important, after the elections, King Hassan offered the opposition Democratic Bloc 19 ministerial posts in the new government.

But this milestone in the development of Moroccan political liberalization did not mean that the parliamentary dominance of neoliberal forces had in fact been curtailed in any substantive sense. On the contrary, the subsequent indirect poll of 1993, like those of 1984 and 1977, ensured a conservative royalist majority. Once again, the neoliberal Constitutional Union emerged as the largest single party, and the four right-wing parties of the royalist Entente obtained 154 seats against 115 seats for the four opposition parties of the Democratic Bloc. Though not commanding a majority of the 333 seats, the Entente has been able to rely on smaller right-wing parties to railroad legislation through the parliament. For example, in November 1993, it easily pushed through a conservative government economic program, with a vote of 202 in favor, to only 118 against.[14]

Similarly, though offering the opposition greater opportunities for participation in the cabinet, the king's effort to tempt the Democratic Bloc into a 'government of renewal and change' did not signal an abatement of the regime's commitment to neoliberal development. Rather, the king qualified his offer in a manner that forced the opposition to reject it. First, technocratic royalists would have continued to control the key ministries of finance, interior, justice, and foreign affairs. Second, the Democratic Bloc would have had to agree to adhere to 'tight fiscal and monetary policies.' Consequently, the opposition refused to join an administration controlled by the establishment and committed to neoliberal orthodoxy.[15]

Following the creation in 1996 of a directly elected 325-member Chamber of Representatives, the opposition again did well in the parliamentary election. By winning 56 seats – more than any other party – the left-of-center Socialist Union of Popular Forces (USFP) was able to lead the new government. But the apparent USFP victory did little to recast the ideological or practical orientation of the new parliament and government. Conservative forces once again won most of the parliamentary seats. Equally important, the monarchy has tightly controlled the cabinet composition and policy orientation of the USFP-led government. The king has appointed key ministers, and has required the new government to stay on the path of neoliberal economic reform. In sum, right-wing electoral and political dominance has not declined in any substantive sense in Morocco.

Likewise, in 1984 semi-rentier Egypt designed a political opening that exemplified that country's approach to economic reform for much of the 1980s and 1990s. The regime highlighted its relatively populist policies, by preventing the leftist opposition from obtaining any parliament seats, and by ensuring that the neoliberal New Wafd would be the only parliamentary opposition. By 1987, the government was still relying on its exogenous resources to forestall serious economic reform; and parliamentary elections that year once again installed neoliberal groups in a dominant position in the parliamentary opposition.

Here the regime sought to incorporate into the parliament a somewhat more diverse opposition than it did in 1984. Nevertheless, among these groups, the New Wafd remained the best-represented party, winning 10 percent of the vote and 36 seats. In 1987, as in 1984, the New Wafd was the only individual party able to overcome the 8 percent electoral threshold imposed by the regime. (The party's High Commision therefore rejected an alliance with other opposition parties before the 1987 elections.) Also winning seats was a tripartite coalition – including the Muslim Brotherhood and the Liberal and Socialist Labor Parties – which won 17.05 percent of the votes and 56 seats. Despite being called the Socialist Labor Party Alliance, this coalition was in fact controlled by neoliberal forces, especially Islamist ones. Most of the members of the Alliance were Muslim Brothers backed by huge Islamist finance houses in the Gulf, and espousing economic policies that were every bit as conservative as those of the New Wafd. The Liberal Party also endorsed neoliberal development policies, and the Socialist Labor Party was forced to back away from its center-left policies. Equally important, as in the 1984 elections, leftist opposition parties were unable to win any representation. In the end, the 1987 elections extended a policy that originated in Sadat's approach to the opposition in the late 1970s: the NDP permitted a much greater articulation of interests among the rightist opposition than among the leftist opposition.[16]

By the early 1990s, the regime began to implement serious reforms – albeit ones that have not matched the scope and severity of those in the minimally rentier states – in exchange for a truly extraordinary foreign aid package that addressed Western geopolitical concerns. At that point, having taken an unusual path to a limited economic neoliberalism, the regime decided that it no longer needed a parliamentary opposition and closed much of the political space. As described in Chapter 5, the result has been the rollback of Egyptian political liberalization, including the increasing irrelevance of the parliament and the demise of any serious opposition.

The resumption of the Kuwaiti parliamentary process in 1992 merely reinforced the anti-bourgeois trend that had existed in the polity since its independence in 1961. In the 1981 and 1985 elections, prominent merchants secured two seats. Relations between the state and the merchants declined throughout the 1980s. In the 1992 and 1996 elections, though many prominent merchants were candidates, only one succeeded in obtaining a parliamentary seat.[17] Through the late 1990s the Kuwaiti parliament remained a distinctly populist force in Kuwaiti politics.

THE FOUR CASES IN REGIONAL PERSPECTIVE

I have argued that the four cases of this study are exemplars of their respective categories, in that each regime has given bourgeois and center-right groups a well-defined electoral position: either dominant, oppositional, or peripheral. The results of the other regional political openings are compatible with my hypotheses, though they may not correspond to the parameters of my framework as clearly as the four cases that I have chosen.

In themselves, Turkey, Morocco, Egypt, and Kuwait contain well over half of the regional population living in countries that experienced political openings in the 1980s and 1990s.[18] In this sense, one framework describes a predominant development trend following the onset of the debt crisis and the global push toward neoliberalism. Still, in the following sections, I apply my hypotheses to other Middle Eastern countries and reflect on regional trends in economic and political reform.

Before reflecting on other political openings, however, I shall explain why I am not applying my hypothesis about political reform to several Middle Eastern cases. Above all, I am considering cases in which the regime has allowed a genuine electoral competition for at least some of the parliamentary seats. Consequently, cases such as Syria, Iraq, and even Tunisia are excluded.

Likewise, this study has assumed the existence of coherent and stable state structures, which are able in general to formulate and implement basic development policies. I am not discussing, therefore, developments in Algeria, Yemen, Sudan, and Lebanon which are exceptions to the regional norms of state cohesion and stability.[19] Thus, the following sections focus on elections in Iran and Jordan.

ELECTORAL POLITICS IN POST-REVOLUTION IRAN: A VIGOROUS POPULISM

My hypotheses would predict that a vigorous populism and statism would dominate the electoral politics of post-revolution Iran, since that state has received most of its revenues from oil exports. In the event, the regime has ensured that forces espousing an anti-Western form of statist and populist intervention have dominated the parliamentary elections held in 1980, 1984, 1988, and 1992. Indeed, the religious hard-liners who have dominated most of Iranian parliamentary life have often embraced policies diametrically opposed to the prescriptions of the international neoliberal orthodoxy.

This populist pattern was firmly established in the 1980 founding elections of the Islamic Republic. In early 1980, the regime faced several crises, as tensions increased with Iraq, as an international boycott pushed the economy further into crisis, and as the regime struggled against its domestic and international enemies. The ruling clerics, headed by Ayatollah Ruholla Khomeini, promised a fair and open polling. But in fact religious screening committees carefully excluded parliamentary candidates – and secularists in particular – who did not sympathize with the goals of the regime. Consequently, a hard-line Islamist coalition led by the Islamic Republican Party (IRP) swept the May elections. The urban poor were the key social base of the IRP (until its dissolution in 1987).[20] It won roughly 60 percent of the seats, while supporters of the relatively moderate leader Bani Sadr obtained perhaps 20 percent of the seats.[21]

In turn, the IRP adopted Ayatollah Khomeini's revolutionary approach to development. Above all, it sought to foster Iranian autarky through the severing of all links with the international banking system.[22] As opposed to the neoliberal movement toward increasing global economic integration, the IRP adopted policies that attempted to isolate the Iranian economy and end the influence of foreign capital. Equally striking were the IRP's other development policies and its response to the economic crisis caused by Iran's war with Iraq and international isolation. The IRP passed legislation calling for extensive nationalizations (which had begun in 1979), rigorous state control over trade, and intensive state intervention in agriculture. Especially notable in 1980 and 1981 were the nationalization of the banking system and the proposed redistribution of land and wealth, which targeted large landowners and capitalists. Meanwhile, the IRP pushed for workers' ownership of industry and an increase in wages and benefits. Naturally enough, this approach alienated much of the merchant and business classes, causing tremendous capital flight.[23]

The regime found the implementation of radical policies such as land reform extremely difficult. Yet through the 1980s, it adhered to its ideology, even as the war continued to devastate the economy and to claim half of all state revenues. Before the parliamentary elections in early 1984, the parliament passed more reforms, including new controls over the banking system, the nationalization of foreign trade, the enforcement of more land reform, and the imposition of protective labor laws.[24]

In the 1984 elections, clerics monopolized the lists of candidates even more than in 1980. Only one in three candidates was allowed to participate in the elections. Predictably, the IRP swept the elections and became the only coherent group in the new assembly. All other important political factions were banned from the polling, and Dr Mehdi Barzagan's Freedom Party boycotted the competition. Subsequently, no independent voice existed in the new parliament.[25] In the mid-1980s, responding to pressures from bazaaris and the private sector in general, the regime at times permitted free trade and backed away from its radical reforms.[26] But in early 1988, as parliamentary elections again loomed, Khomeini aggressively reinforced the dominance of the radical Islamist wing. He weakened the Council of Guardians (which had interfered with the implementation of populist policies), called for the expansion of radical Islamic economic programs, and railed against bazaari and private-sector resistance to reform.[27]

Though the IRP was dissolved in 1987, the regime easily maintained the parliamentary dominance of radical Islamic factions, who won 160 out of 260 assembly seats in 1988. (Screening committees again systematically excluded regime opponents.) Instead of the IRP, two new parliamentary factions emerged: the Tehran Militant Clerics, who were radical and favored state control over all aspects of social life; and the Tehran Militant Clergy Association, which increasingly opposed state intervention in economy and society.

The balance between these two factions began to tip in favor of the latter, following the death of Khomeini and the rise of Hashemi Rafsanjani to the presidency in July 1989. That year, facing the daunting prospects of postwar reconstruction, Rafsanjani declared his intention of implementing a Western-style economic reform program that effected high growth and mobilized foreign assistance. Because of clerical opposition, however, that reform program has been extremely slow, intermittent and limited in scope. Populist policies remained vigorous, as radicals pushed the government to double subsidies for essential foods and goods in 1990–1.[28] Indeed, until 1992, the parliament remained in 'the stranglehold of the radicals' who stymied serious reforms and threatened to rally the masses against Rafsanjani's programs.[29]

Prospects for Western-style reforms seemed to improve, when alleged supporters and sympathizers of Rafsanjani won 70 percent of the parliament's seats in elections in May 1992. The main reformist achievement of Rafsanjani was the relinking of Iran to the international economic system. To this end, his government effected in 1993 a 95.6 percent devaluation of the Iranian rial through the partial unification of the country's three main exchange rates. That devaluation hurt the poor. But on the whole, Rafsanjani has never been able to implement a consistent and far-reaching reform program – mainly because hard-liners in the parliament and throughout the government oppose such reforms, or at any rate fear popular upheaval.[30]

Here the battle over subsidies has become pivotal. On the recommendation of the IMF and the World Bank in 1993, Rafsanjani signaled his intention to reduce the state's extensive consumer subsidies. In response, anti-Western parliamentary forces (loyal to Iran's supreme religious leader, Ayatollah Ali Khamenei) engineered a reversal of Iran's weak version of reforms and austerity in early 1994. These groups succeeded in expanding a range of consumptive and populist policies, including a tremendous increase in basic consumer subsidies.[31] Similarly, the 1996 elections left forces opposing neo-liberal economic reform in firm control of the parliament. Even the ascent of the relatively reform-minded Muhamad Khatami to the presidency in 1997 failed to reorient the developmental policies of the Iranian state.

In the end, despite having a war-ravaged economy, Iran's parliamentary politics has suggested a vigorous rent-based populism and an extremely low commitment to economic reform. Further, like highly rentier Kuwait, the Iranian state has tended to be anti-capitalist in its approach to electoral politics. Accordingly, its efforts at neoliberal economic reform have paled in comparison to those of Middle Eastern states with fewer exogenous resources.

JORDAN: MOVING TOWARD THE MINIMALLY RENTIER POLE

In Jordan, a severe drop in exogenous resources prompted the regime to create one of the Arab world's most far-reaching political openings, as I explained in Chapter 5. Jordan has resembled the minimally rentier Moroccan case, in that the coincidence of political and economic crises generated a substantive process of political liberalization. In a word, powerful crises compelled the regimes to seek a far-reaching electoral legitimation.

More broadly, Jordan resembles Turkey and Morocco, in that a lack of exogenous resources (during the late 1980s) induced a severe economic crisis and left Jordan with no option but the implementation of an orthodox restructuring program. As well, Jordan mirrors Morocco and Turkey in its favoring of center-right forces in the electoral parliament, though here the Jordanian process has been less sweeping and formalized than that of the archetypal minimally rentier states.

While conforming to the minimally rentier pattern in critical respects, the Jordanian trajectory did resemble the semi-rentier category in the early and middle 1980s. Before the economic crisis of the late 1980s, Jordan received considerably higher levels of exogenous rents as a percentage of state revenue than did Morocco and Turkey. That is, *before* the onset of the foreign aid crisis of the late 1980s, Jordan resembled semi-rentier Egypt, in that both received significant exogenous rents and were reluctant to reform their economies. Whereas Morocco and Turkey experienced economic crises in the early 1980s, Jordan did not have one until most of its exogenous resource dramatically evaporated in the mid- and late-1980s. Like Egypt, therefore, it was relatively slow in implementing economic reform – with both countries being what Stallings would call 'late' reformers.

In the end, as argued in Chapter 5, the Jordanian and Egyptian development paths diverged. Egypt was able to avoid the minimally rentier crisis, mainly because it had more reliable and diversified sources of exogenous revenues. In the late 1980s, those revenues allowed Egypt to avoid the kind of fiscal crisis that compelled Jordan to reach a sweeping accommodation with international financial institutions. Here geopolitics enabled Egypt to maintain its access to critical levels of foreign exchange. Further, in 1990–91, because of the Gulf crisis and war, Egypt maintained its leverage *vis-à-vis* its international donors, and its enhanced bargaining position enabled it to avoid such a sweeping process of reform, austerity, and political liberalization. As I argued in Chapter 5, Egypt liberalized economically *in exchange for* an unprecedented exogenous windfall, which in turn undercut the regime's movement toward political liberalization.

By contrast, concerning both political and economic reform, Jordan had come to resemble the minimally rentier states in critical respects. Here the regimes opened their political systems soon after reaching watershed agreements with the international creditor community. In sum, in the cases of Morocco, Turkey, and Jordan, low levels of exogenous revenues have led to a tripartite process: first, the occurrence of a crippling political-economic crisis; second, the regime's relatively swift and dynamic adoption of economic neo-liberalism; and third, the conduct of a political opening that sought to legitimate the neoliberal development model. Morocco and Turkey are exemplars of this minimally rentier pattern, though Jordan also strongly mirrors it.

MULTIPARTISM AND POLITICAL LIBERALIZATION IN MINIMALLY RENTIER STATES

Multipartism represents the substantive and risky dimension of Middle Eastern political openings. In the regional context of liberalizing authoritarianism, it suggests a substantive parliamentary accommodation with opposition forces. Ideally, multipartism implies some kind of power-sharing, by curbing the power of the ruling party and enabling opponents to participate in some aspect of the policy-making process. Presumably, this process has the potential to evolve some day into a genuine democratization. Moreover, in the short term, multipartism enables opposition groups to protect newly extended political liberties, including freedoms of movement, speech, petition, dissent, and so forth. As such, the regime sanctions and institutionalizes a delimitation of its power. Substantive multipartism emerges, because the regime believes that it signifies the best strategy for the forging of some kind of 'democratic bargain' with bourgeois groups contributing resources to the development program and with popular sectors bearing the brunt of economic austerity. Its development in Jordan and Morocco has followed the onset of economic crisis and the regime's acceptance of far-reaching neoliberal reforms.

The development of multipartism, in an important sense, increases the vulnerability and the accountability of the regime to popular pressure. In assessing the current wave of regional political openings, analysts have considered multipartism to be pivotal in the regime's political progress. Conversely, they have considered developments in Tunisia and Egypt to be so disappointing, precisely because the regimes were unwilling to provide for substantive oppositional activity.

Typically, the nature of the crisis dictates the extent to which regime elites are willing to permit liberalization and democratization. A manageable crisis or challenge tends to translate into a highly limited or controlled liberalization. A far-reaching crisis – a near collapse of the economy, for example – limits the ability of the regime elites to control the political opening, and gives more leverage to an opposition seeking genuine democratization. The upshot here is that among Arab states sustained multipartist parliaments exist *only* in minimally rentier states, that is, Jordan and Morocco. A third minimally rentier state – Tunisia – has become increasingly liberalized since 1980 largely because of its economic troubles, even though its progress overall has been disappointing. In the rest of the Middle East, prospects for greater political liberalization have been rather poor in recent years, as I discuss below.

I have argued that different kinds of crises or challenges are more apt to lead to substantive political liberalization. Whereas severe domestic threats, especially economic crises, have prompted regimes to construct substantive political openings, milder challenges, such as attempts to acquire foreign aid, have encouraged regimes to develop electoral experiments that offer opposition groups less substantive accommodations and have more of a propagandistic intent. Here I contrast the Egyptian elections of 1990, which effectively constricted the existing electoral opening and seemed to be designed to satisfy Western donors, and the increases in Jordanian and Moroccan liberalization following economic crises in those countries.

In the end, minimally rentier status seems to have been a sufficient condition for a process of economic crisis, neoliberal reform, and the favoring of a center-right bourgeoisie in the parliament. At the same time, as the Tunisian case shows, minimally rentier status seems to have been a necessary, but not a sufficient condition for the implementation of a substantive multipartism.

This distinction stems from the fact that economic resources closely condition the selection of development and electoral coalition strategies, with regimes opting for heterodox populist policies whenever possible. The extent of political liberalization is a thornier issue. It roughly reflects the severity of the crises facing the regimes. Only those states experiencing powerful economic problems – those at or near the minimally rentier pole – are likely to seek the implementation of the multipartist 'democratic bargain.' Yet the emergence of a substantive political liberalization ultimately hinges upon the strategic – and contingent – decisions of policy-makers. Of course, the selection of development strategies and the favoring of electoral coalitions also signify contingent strategic decisions, but ones that are more directly and sharply circumscribed by the availability of economic resources.

In all of the minimally rentier cases, observers noted that the adoption of neoorthodoxy was seemingly 'inevitable' given the state's resource gap. In turn, to legitimate the new economic model, the regime had no choice but to engineer a parliamentary dominance of the center-right. All the while, that same international environment did not insist on the implementation of substantive political liberalization. Of course, Western patrons sometimes applauded movements in that direction; and a form of democratic bargain made strategic sense in most of these situations. But in itself, a state resource gap did not necessarily mean that a significant political opening would enhance the regime's control over the polity. Such an eventuality hinged on the structure and resilience of the regime and opposition. Above all, regime elites did not know whether they would be able to control opposition groups and the electoral process in general.

In short, the solution to the foreign exchange crisis of the minimally rentier state was relatively clear, to the extent that a neoliberal alliance provided resources that bridged a yawning budgetary gap. Meanwhile, the logic of the 'democratic bargain' was somewhat less compelling – its benefits to regime security were much less certain.

THE RELATIONSHIP BETWEEN POLITICAL AND ECONOMIC REFORMS IN REGIONAL AND GLOBAL PERSPECTIVE

Wide variations in the availability of exogenous resources have stratified the trajectories of regional political reforms.

Rent-poor regimes often had no choice but to impose substantive economic reform. In exchange for the imposition of economic austerity, these regimes sought an electoral legitimation of their rule. This act, above all, was an attempt to alleviate popular dissatisfaction and to mobilize support for the development model. Therefore, in minimally rentier countries, a close association exists between economic reform and political liberalization.[32] In a word, far-reaching economic crisis has provided the most propitious context for meaningful political liberalization in the Middle East. Such a crisis, by and large, has been most likely to occur in those Middle Eastern states commanding relatively few exogenous resources.

Rent-rich regimes have not been compelled to impose far-reaching economic austerity, and therefore have had little incentive to offer their populations any electoral legitimation of their rule. That is, extremely high levels of exogenous revenues militate against both economic and political liberalization, as is evident in Iraq, Libya, and all of the Gulf monarchies (except Kuwait).

In sum, the correlation between political liberalization and exogenous rent levels is of course rough – rougher at any rate, than the correlation between rent levels and economic liberalization. The important exceptions to the regional rentier paradigm are Tunisia and Syria and Iran, which are less democratic than one would expect, and Kuwait and Iran, which are more democratic than one would expect.

Of course, levels of exogenous revenues do not determine all instances and facets of regional political development, despite having created critical overall trends. The rentier state hypothesis indicates why the rent-poor tend to be more democratic and the rent-rich tend to be less so; and it has been insightfully applied to particular instances in which exogenous revenues have reordered political life. But exceptional cases illustrate that revenue structures affect, but do not determine whether or not regimes liberalize. Key overriding factors often relate to the nature of the regimes and oppositions. Why, for example, has a relatively rent-poor Syria been less liberalized than relatively rent-rich Kuwait in recent years? A relatively liberalized Kuwaiti polity grew out of the political activities of an usually strong and cohesive bourgeoisie in the pre-independence era; and the usually centralized, exclusionary, sectarian nature of the Syrian regime helps to account for the complete absence of political liberalization in that country. That is, Kuwait is unusually democratic and Syria is unusually authoritarian, in relation to their state revenue structures.

Despite these exceptions, the varying availability of exogenous revenues has created two diverging development possibilities for most regional states. One tendency includes rent-poor countries that have developed relatively liberalized political and economic systems. The other trajectory includes

rent-rich countries that have averted both political and economic liberalizations. Both versions are authoritarian. But the rent-poor model features
limited political liberties and economic neoliberalism, while the rent-rich
one offers economic populism and political repression. Here in global
perspective, the Middle East suggests distinct development patterns, as I argue
below.

A GLOBAL PERSPECTIVE: A 'DEMOCRATIC BARGAIN' OR THE 'SEQUENCING' OF REFORMS?

No consensus exists on whether political and economic reforms are
essentially compatible in the Middle East. Kiren Aziz Chaudhry suggests
that even limited political *liberalization* undermines economic reform.[33]
By contrast, Richards and Waterbury argue that economic reform and
limited political liberalization may well complement one another, 'in the
sense that new economic and professional interests will want to organize to
protect and extend their advantages.'[34] A few scholars such as Patrick Clawson
are even more sanguine. They point out that certain states outside the region
have recently benefited from 'democratic bargains,' in which carefully
controlled political openings have allowed for genuine democratic
participation, and at the same time have protected austere economic policies.
They have been impressed by an 'Eastern European' model, in which
sweeping economic reform and genuine democratization have occurred
simultaneously. Indeed, they have suggested that the implementation of
economic reform offers the best prospect for democratization in the Middle
East.[35]

Does the process of economic crisis and reform, then, promote
renewed political repression, limited political liberalization, or genuine
democratization? The empirical reality, of course, demonstrates the close
affinity of political and economic liberalizations. But, as I argue below, recent
comparativist literature helps to explain why rent-poor states exhibit a
distinctive combination of liberalized authoritarianism and neoliberal
stabilization. Democratization, on this logic, would destabilize economic
reforms, whereas the roll back of political liberalization would destabilize the
regime.

A body of comparativist literature in the 1970s and 1980s emphasized that
authoritarian regimes tended to be better than democracies at modernizing
the economy and at managing and surviving economic crises. Much of this
literature assumed that developing countries undergoing structural economic
reform tended to become increasingly authoritarian.[36] Many authors argued
that strong and stable authoritarian rule was the best form of governance for

Third World countries experiencing rapid development.[37] Other scholars have argued, more specifically, that political reform and economic liberalization are unlikely to coexist, in so far as economic austerity tends to shrink the popular constituencies of liberalizing regimes.[38]

Assessing the current trends toward political liberalization and democratization around the world, recent studies have questioned these assumptions. Karen Remmer, for example, shows that democratic and authoritarian regimes of Latin America were, by and large, equally successful in imposing austerity and IMF-sponsored stabilization.[39] Stephan Haggard argues that particular democracies stabilized and adjusted rather well, whereas some authoritarian regimes did quite poorly in the 1980s.[40]

In comparing 25 developing countries from different regions, Haggard and Kaufman argue that while regime type is not 'irrelevant,' one must seek 'nuanced' distinctions '*within* the authoritarian and democratic categories.'[41] Having distinguished among 'new democracies,' 'continuous democracies,' and 'continuous authoritarian regimes,' they conclude that continuous democratic and authoritarian regimes were, by and large, equally successful in implementing economic reform in the 1980s. They conclude, moreover, that certain kinds of democracies and authoritarian regimes are more capable than others at imposing austerity, stabilization, and adjustment. In particular, the new or transitional democracies as a group had less success in managing economic reform and maintaining stable policies than did the established regimes. These countries in fact tended to pursue expansionist policies, both in comparison to their past policies and to those of the other countries in the sample.[42]

Like Barbara Stallings, Haggard and Kaufman suggest that 'strong' and stable regimes, be they democratic or authoritarian, are better able to formulate and implement reform programs. Key characteristics of that strength include regime continuity, high technical and bureaucratic capacities, and policy-makers who are largely insulated from distributive pressures and domestic political forces as they implement economic reform.[43]

Thus, in the long term, one might expect a version of the sequencing that Haggard and Kaufman have observed in a range of countries struggling with political and economic reforms.[44] That logic suggests that regimes may implement sweeping economic reforms, or may permit full-blown democratization. But the contradiction between these two goals means that in all likelihood they will not pursue both at the same time. Here it seems that rulers of minimally rentier states have sought to reconcile electoral legitimation and policy-making autonomy. Economic austerity and stabilization have proved to be compatible with a liberalized authoritarianism in Morocco and Jordan. In these cases, it is doubtful that a genuine democratization would provide for governing structures that would have the autonomy and capacity to maintain neoliberal development policies. In all minimally rentier cases, regimes have relied on exclusionary mechanisms to silence popular sectors whose wages have plummeted and whose tax burdens have risen. Evidence from all countries suggests a pervasive popular dislike of economic orthodoxy. Consequently, in the short run, an *incomplete* democratization has a compelling logic. The provision of some political liberties burnishes the image of the regime at home and abroad, and coopts the cooperation of key players, specifically a center-right bourgeoisie. Meanwhile, authoritarian controls ensure the implementation of an unpopular development plan considered essential to economic viability.

Here the rent-poor model of liberalized authoritarianism and neoliberal economics will be a plausible governing strategy until the regimes believe that they are able to relax economic austerity. That means that the current rent-poor model may well endure for the next decade or so.

And what in coming years would prevent beleaguered regimes from reversing political liberalization, as they are forced to attempt destabilizing reorganizations of their economies? In the long run, as simple rentier theory would have it, the reversal of political liberalization is unlikely in increasingly production-oriented polities. In a word, the collapse of exogenous resources means that politics increasingly revolves around taxation and representation. In rent-poor states, therefore, attempts at wholesale reintroduction of repression might destabilize the regimes. Genuine democratization, conversely, is a long-term possibility, but only at a time when these regimes need not rely on authoritarian controls to maintain stabilization and adjustment policies. Plainly, democratization and orthodox neoliberalism are incompatible in the Middle East.

How, then, should Western donors approach the issue of political and economic reform in the Middle East? The aim of this book has not been an evaluation of the merits or demerits of neoliberal reform. But this analysis has underscored the contradictions between political and economic reforms in the Middle East. It has also emphasized neoliberalism's lack of popular legitimacy, which is rooted in the reality that, by and large, this new global economic regime has increased poverty and inequality in the region.[45] For the long term, so long as the dimension of social justice is ignored, the applications of strict orthodoxy (as mandated by the Western powers) may well lead to greater instability in the Middle East. The glimmer of hope here is that international donors – and the World Bank in particular – are gradually recognizing that economic policies in non-Western societies will necessarily provide social justice. A more flexible, heterodox and humane conception of development would ease some of the policy dilemmas facing Middle Easterners.

NOTES

1. Barbara Stallings, 'International Influence on Economic Policy: Debt, Stabilization, and Structural Reform,' in Stephan Haggard and Robert Kaufman (eds), *The Politics of Economic Adjustment*, Princeton, NJ: Princeton University Press, 1992.
2. Guillermo O'Donnell and Philippe Schmitter, *Transitions from Authoritarian Rule: Tentative Conclusions about Uncertain Democracies*, Baltimore, MD: Johns Hopkins University Press, 1986, p. 71.
3. See, for example, Muharrem Tunay, 'The New Turkish Right's Attempt at Hegemony,' in Atila Erlap, Muharrem Tunay, and Birol Yesilada (eds), *The Political and Economic Transformation of Turkey*, Westport, CT: Praeger, 1993.
4. Andrew Mango, 'The Social Democratic Populist Party, 1983-1989,' in Metin Heper and Jacob Landau (eds), *Political Parties and Democracy in Turkey*, London: I.B. Tauris, 1991.
5. John Waterbury, 'Export-led Growth and the Center-right Coalition in Turkey,' in Tevfik Nas and Mehmet Odekon (eds), *Economics and Politics of Turkish Liberalization*, Bethlehem, PA: Lehigh University Press, 1992, p. 65.
6. For an emphasis of the importance of coalitions in Egyptian reforms, see Raymond Hinnebusch, 'The Politics of Egyptian Economic Reform,' *Third World Quarterly*, 14(1) (1993), 159-71.
7. See my discussion in Chapter 5. Alan Richards and John Waterbury make this comparison in *A Political Economy of the Middle East: State, Class and Economic Development*, Boulder, CO: Westview Press, 1990, pp. 284-5.
8. Clement Henry Dodd, *The Crisis of Turkish Democracy*, 2nd edn, Cambridgeshire: Eothen Press, 1990, p. 98.
9. Miles Kahler, 'External Influence, Conditionality, and the Politics of Adjustment,' in Haggard and Kaufman (eds), *Politics of Economic Adjustment*, p. 111.
10. John Waterbury, 'Export-led Growth and the Center-right Coalition in Turkey,' in ibid.
11. Stephan Haggard and Robert Kaufman, 'Economic Adjustment in New Democracies,' in John Waterbury (ed.), *The Political Economy of Public Sector Reform and Privatization*, Boulder, CO: Westview Press, 1990, p. 59.
12. See, for example, Tunay, 'New Turkish Right,' or Waterbury, 'Export-led Growth.'
13. *The Middle East Review 1995*, London: Kogan Page, 1994, p. 68.
14. The Economist Intelligence Unit, *Morocco Country Report*, London: The Economist, 1994, First Quarter, 1994, p. 2; and Third Quarter, 1994, p. 8.
15. Ibid.
16. Mona Makram Ebeid, 'Political Opposition in Egypt: Democratic Myth or Reality?', *Middle East Journal*, 43(3) (1989), 429.
17. The Economist Intelligence Unit, *Kuwait Country Profile 1994-95*, London: The Economist, 1995, p. 5.
18. *Handbook of Economic Statistics, 1990*, Washington, DC: Directorate of Intelligence, Central Intelligence Agency.
19. Concerning, for example, the landmark 1993 Yemeni elections: from the 1990 unification until the 1994 civil war, factionalism had paralyzed an already weak and truncated Yemeni state. Consequently, between 1992 and 1994, the government was unable even to formulate an economic program (see *Middle East Review, 93-94*, pp.138-9). Similarly, in recent years the Algerian and Lebanese regimes have been too weak to formulate or impose a coherent development strategy.
20. Shahrough Akhavi, 'Iran,' in Frank Tachau (ed.), *Political Parties of the Middle East and North Africa*, Westport, CT: Greenwood Press, 1994, p. 157.
21. Economist Intelligence Unit, *Quarterly Economic Review of Iran*, 3rd Quarter, 1980, p. 5.
22. Ibid., 1st Quarter 1981, p. 12.
23. Economist Intelligence Unit, *Iran: Annual Supplement, 1980-81*, London: The Economist, p. 11.
24. Economist Intelligence Unit, *Quarterly Economic Review of Iran*, 1984, no. 1, p. 4.
25. Ibid., p. 10.
26. Ibid.

27. Ibid., 1988, no. 2, pp. 11-13.
28. Ibid., 1990, no. 3, p. 1.
29. Ibid., 1990, no. 1, p. 12.
30. Ibid., 1993, no. 2, p. 17.
31. Chris Hedges, 'Islamic Hardliners Said to Gain Ground in Iran,' *New York Times*, August 3, 1994, A3.
32. Patrick Clawson, for example, argues that economic reform causes political liberalization in his chapter 'What's so Good about Stability?' in Henri J. Barkey (ed.), *The Politics of Economic Reform in the Middle East*, New York: St Martin's Press, 1992.
33. Kiren Aziz Chaudhry, 'On the Way to Market: Economic Liberalization and Iraq's Invasion of Kuwait,' *Middle East Report*, no. 170 (May/June 1991).
34. Richards and Waterbury, *Political Economy of the Middle East*, p. 436.
35. See, for example, Clawson, 'What's so Good about Stability?'.
36. Guillermo O'Donnel, *Modernization and Bureaucratic Authoritarianism*, Berkeley, CA: Institute of International Studies, University of California, 1979.
37. Samuel Huntington, *Political Order in Changing Societies*, New Haven, CT: Yale University Press, 1968.
38. See, for example, Chaudhry, 'On the Way to Market.'
39. Karen Remmer, 'The Politics of Economic Stabilization: IMF Standby Programs in Latin America, 1954-84,' *Comparative Politics*, 19(1) (October 1986), 1-24.
40. Stephan Haggard, 'The Politics of Adjustment: Lessons from the IMF's Extended Fund Facility,' in Miles Kahler (ed.), *The Politics of International Debt*, Ithaca, NY: Cornell University Press, 1986.
41. Haggard and Kaufman, *Politics of Economic Adjustment*, p. 59.
42. Ibid.
43. Ibid.
44. Stephan Haggard and Robert Kaufman, 'Economic Adjustment and the Prospects for Democracy,' in their *Politics of Economic Adjustment*, p. 332.
45. See, for example, Karen Pfeifer, 'How Tunisia, Morocco, Jordan and even Egypt Became IMF "Success Stories" in the 1990s,' *Middle East Report*, Spring 1999, 23-33.

Bibliography

Abazza, Ibrahim Dessouki (1984a), 'The State ... Is a Private Sector!' *Al Wafd* (Cairo), November 1, 6 [in Arabic].

Abazza, Ibrahim (1984b), 'Congratulations, Wafd,' *Al Wafd* (Cairo), June 7, 3 [in Arabic].

Al Ahram (Cairo) (1984), January–June issues [in Arabic].

Ames, Barry (1987), *Political Survival*, Berkeley, CA: University of California Press.

Anderson, Lisa (1987), 'The State in the Middle East and North Africa,' *Comparative Politics*, 20 (October), 1–13.

Anderson, Lisa (1990), 'Policy-making and Theory Building: American Political Science and the Islamic Middle East,' in Hisham Shirabi (ed.), *Theory, Politics and the Arab World*, New York: Routledge.

Anderson, Lisa (1991), 'Absolutism and the Resilience of Monarchy in the Middle East,' *Political Science Quarterly*, 106(1), 1–16.

Arat, Yesim (1991), 'Social Change and the 1983 Governing Elite in Turkey,' in Mubeccel Kiral (ed.), *Structural Change in Turkish Society*, Bloomington, IN: Indiana University Press.

Assiri, Abdul-Reida and al-Monoufi, Kamal (1988), 'Kuwait's Political Elite: the Cabinet,' *Middle East Journal*, 42, 48–58.

Al Bahairi, Mustapha (1984), 'Reactions to the Elections in Britain,' *Al Wafd* (Cairo), June 14, 10.

Bahbouhi, T. (ed.) (1985), *Parliamentary Experience in Morocco*, Casablanca: Les Editions Toubkal.

Barakat, Halim (1985), *Contemporary North Africa: Issues of Development and Integration*, Washington, DC: Center for Contemporary Arab Studies.

Barkey, Henri J. (1989), 'State Autonomy and the Crisis of Import Substitution,' *Comparative Political Studies*, 2 (October), 291–314.

Barkey, Henri J. (1992a), *The State and the Industrialization Crisis in Turkey*, New York: St Martin's Press.

Barkey, Henri J. (ed.) (1992b), *The Politics of Economic Reform in the Middle East*, New York: St Martin's Press.

Beblawi, Hazem and Luciani, Giacomo (eds) (1987), *Nation, State and Integration in the Arab World*, vol. 2: *The Rentier State*, London: Croom Helm.

Bermeo, Nancy (1990), 'Rethinking Regime Change,' *Comparative Politics*, 22 (April), 359–77.

Bianchi, Robert (1989), *Unruly Corporatism: Associational Life in Twentieth-century Egypt*, London: Oxford University Press.

Bill, James and Springborg, Robert (1990), *Politics in the Middle East*, 3rd edn, New York: HarperCollins.

Brynen, Rex, Korany, Bahgat and Noble, Paul (1996), *Political Liberalization and Democratization in the Arab World*, vols 1 and 2, Boulder, CO: Lynne Reinner.

Brumberg, Daniel (1991), 'Prospects for a "Democratic Bargain" in the Middle East,' a paper presented to a National Endowment for Democracy seminar, Washington, DC. April.

Brumberg, Daniel (1992), 'Survival Strategies vs. Democratic Bargains: the Politics of Economic Reform in Contemporary Egypt,' in Henri J. Barkey (ed.), *The Politics of Economic Reform in the Middle East*, New York: St Martin's Press.

Brouwer, Imco (1999), 'Civil Society Assistance to the Arab World,' unpublished paper.

Central Intelligence Agency, Directorate of Intelligence (various), *Handbook of Economic Statistics*, Washington, DC: US Government Printing Office.

Chatelus, Michael (1987), 'Policies for Development: Attitudes toward Industry and Services,' in Beblawi and Luciani (eds), *Nation, State and Integration in the Arab World*, vol. 2: *The Rentier State*, London: Croom Helm.

Chaudhry, Kiren Aziz (1989), 'The Price of Oil Wealth: Business and State in Labor Remittance and Oil Economies,' *International Organization*, 43 (Winter), 101–45.

Chaudhry, Kiren Aziz (1991), 'On the Way to Market: Economic Liberalization and Iraq's Invasion of Kuwait,' *Middle East Report*, 170 (May/June).

Chaudhry, Kiren Aziz (1994), 'Economic Liberalization and the Lineages of the Rentier State,' *Comparative Politics*, (October), 1–25.

Claisse, Alain (1987), 'Makhzen Traditions and Administrative Channels,' in I. William Zartman (ed.), *The Political Economy of Morocco*, Westport, CT: Praeger.

Clawson, Patrick (1992), 'What's So Good about Stability?' in Henri J. Barkey (ed.), *The Politics of Economic Reform in the Middle East*, New York: St Martin's Press.

Clément, Jean François (1986), 'Morocco's Bourgeoisie: Monarchy, State, and Owning Class,' *Middle East Report* (September–October).

Collier, David (ed.) (1979), *The New Authoritarianism in Latin America*, Princeton, NJ: Princeton University Press.

Crystal, Jill (1989), 'Coalitions in Oil Monarchies: Kuwait and Qatar,' *Comparative Politics*, 21 (July).

Crystal, Jill (1990), *Oil and Politics in the Gulf: Rulers and Merchants in Kuwait and Qatar*, Cambridge: Cambridge University Press.

Crystal, Jill (1992), *Kuwait: Transformation of an Oil State*, Boulder, CO: Westview Press.

Dahl, Robert (1973), *Regimes and Oppositions*, New Haven, CT: Yale University Press.

Daher, Ahmed J. and Al-Salem, Faisal (1984), 'Kuwait's Parliamentary Elections,' *Journal of Arab Affairs*, 3, 85–98.

Damis, John (1983), *Conflict in Northwest Africa: The Western Sahara Dispute*, Stanford, CA: Hoover Institution Press.

Dessouki, Ali E. Hillal (1993), 'Assessment of the Legislative Sector in Egypt,' Cairo: USAID.

Delacroix, Jacques (1980), 'The Rentier State in the World System,' *Studies in International Comparative Development*, 15, 3–21.

Diamond, Larry (ed.) (1999), *Developing Democracy: Toward Consolidation*, Baltimore, MD: Johns Hopkins University Press.

Dodd, Christopher H. (1990), *The Crisis of Turkish Democracy*, 2nd edn, Wistow, Cambs.: Eothen Press.

Dornbush, Rudiger and Edwards, Sebastian (eds) (1991), *The Macroeconomics of Populism in Latin America*, Chicago, IL: National Bureau of Economic Research and the University of Chicago Press.

Ebeid, Mona Makram (1989), 'Political Opposition in Egypt: Democratic Myth or Reality?', *Middle East Journal*, 43.

Ebeid, Mona Makram (1994), 'Democratization in Egypt: "The Algeria Complex",' *Middle East Policy*, 3.

The Economist (1984), 'While the Sun Shines, Egypt Knocks Holes in the Roof,' and 'Cash on the Nile,' April 7.

The Economist (1993), 'Egypt: Slowly to Market,' July 24.

The Economist Intelligence Unit (varoius), Annual and quarterly reports on Turkey, Tunisia, Jordan, Iran, Morocco, Egypt, and Kuwait, London: The Economist.

Egyptian Gazette (1993), 'Egypt Opens Wheat Imports to Private Sector,' September 15.

Eickelman, Dale (1986), 'Royal Authority and Religious Legitimacy: Morocco's Elections, 1960–1984,' Myron J. Aronoff (ed.), in *The Frailty of Authority*, New Brunswick, NJ: Transaction Books.

Elon, Amos (1995), 'One Foot on the Moon,' *New York Review of Books*, April 6.

Entellis, John (1989), *Culture and Counterculture in Moroccan Politics*, Boulder, CO: Westview Press.

Erguder, Urstun (1991), 'The Motherland Party, 1983–89,' in Metin Heper and Urstun Erguder (eds), *Political Parties and Democracy in Turkey*, London: I.B. Tauris.

Erguder, Urstun and Hofferbert, Richard (1987), 'Restoration of Democracy in Turkey? Political Reforms and the Elections of 1983,' in Linda Layne (ed.), *Elections in the Middle East: Implications of Recent Trends*, Boulder, CO: Westview Press.

Erlap, Atila, Muharrem Tunay and Birol Yesilada (eds) (1993), *The Political and Socioeconomic Transformation of Turkey*, Westport, CT: Praeger.

Fadil, Mahmud Abdel (1987), 'The Macro-behavior of Oil-rentier States in the Arab Region,' in Hazem Beblawi and Giacomo Luciani (eds), *Nation, State and Integration in the Arab World*. Vol. 2: *The Rentier State*, London: Croom Helm.

Findlay, Anne (1984), 'The Moroccan Economy in the 1970s,' in Richard Lawless and Anne Findlay (eds), *North Africa: Contemporary Politics and Economic Development*, New York: St Martin's Press.

Finkel, Andrew and Sirman, Nukhet (eds) (1990), *Turkish State, Turkish Society*, London: Routledge.

El-Fiqi, Fakhri (1993), 'Growth with a Cost,' *Al-Ahram Weekly*, November 18.

Freedom House (1994), *Freedom in the World: The Annual Survey of Political Rights and Civil Liberties, 1993-94*, Lanham, MD: University Press of America.

Frieden, Jeff (1981), 'Third World Indebted Industrialization: International Finance and State Capital in Mexico, Brazil, Algeria, and South Korea,' *International Organization*, 35, 407–32.

Gause, F. Gregory III (1991), 'Revolutionary Fevers and Regional Contagion: Domestic Structures and the "Export" of Revolution in the Middle East,' *Journal of South Asia and Middle East Studies*, 14(3), 1–23.

Gause, F. Gregory III (1993), *Oil Monarchies*, New York: Council on Foreign Affairs.

Gavrielides, Nicolas (1987), 'Tribal Democracy: the Anatomy of Parliamentary Elections in Kuwait,' in Linda Layne (ed.), *Elections in the Middle East: Implications of Recent Trends*, Boulder, CO: Westview Press.

Al-Gomhuriyah (Cairo) (1984), January–June issues.

Haggard, Stephan (1986), 'The Politics of Adjustment: Lessons from the IMFs Extended Fund Facility,' in Miles Kahler (ed.), *The Politics of International Debt*, Ithaca, NY: Cornell University Press.

Haggard, Stephan and Kaufman, Robert (1989), 'The Politics of Stabilization and Structural Adjustment,' in Jeffrey Sachs (ed.), *Developing Country*

Debt and Economic Performance: The International Financial System, Chicago: University of Chicago Press.

Haggard, Stephan (1992), 'Economic Adjustment and the Prospects for Democracy,' in their *The Politics of Economic Adjustment*, Princeton, NJ: Princeton University Press.

Hale, William (1981), *The Political and Economic Development of Modern Turkey*, London: Croom Helm.

Harik, Iliya (1997), *Economic Policy Reform in Egypt*, Gainsville, FL: University Press of Florida.

Harik, Ilya and Sullivan, Denis (eds) (1992), *Privatization and Liberalization in the Middle East*, Bloomington, IN: Indiana University Press.

Hedges, Chris (1994a), 'Egypt Begins Crackdown on Strongest Opposition Group,' *New York Times*, June 12, A3.

Hedges, Chris (1994b), 'Islamic Hardliners Said to Gain Ground in Iran,' *New York Times*, August 3, A3.

Henry, Clement (1997), *The Mediterranean Debt Crescent*, Cairo: American University of Cairo Press.

Heper, Metin (1985), *The State Tradition in Turkey*, Wistow, Cambs.: Eothen Press.

Heper, Metin and Evin, Ahmet (eds) (1988), *State, Democracy and the Military: Turkey in the 1980s*, New York: Walter de Gruyter.

Heper, Metin and Landau, Jacob (eds) (1991), *Political Parties and Democracy in Turkey*, London: I.B. Tauris.

Heydemann, Steve (1992), 'The Political Logic of Economic Rationality: Selective Stabilization in Syria,' in Henri J. Barkey (ed.), *The Politics of Economic Reform in the Middle East*, New York: St Martin's Press.

Hudson, Michael (1991), 'After the Gulf War: Prospects for Democratization in the Arab World,' *Middle East Journal*, 45(3), (Summer), 407–26.

Huntington, Samuel (1968), *Political Order in Changing Societies*, New Haven, CT: Yale University Press.

Huntington, Samuel (1987), 'The Goals of Development,' in S. Huntington and M. Weiner (eds), *Understanding Political Development*, Boston: Little Brown.

Huntington, Samuel (1991a), 'Democracy's Third Wave,' *Journal of Democracy* (Spring).

Huntington, Samuel (1991b), *The Third Wave: Democratization in the Late Twentieth Century*, Norman, OK: University of Oklahoma Press.

Ibrahim, Saad Eddin (1982), *The New Arab Social Order*, London: Croom Helm.

International Monetary Fund (various), *Government Finance Statistics Yearbooks*, New York: IMF.

Ismael, Jacqueline S. (1993), *Kuwait: Dependency and Class in a Rentier State*, Gainesville, FL: University Press of Florida.

Karl, Terry Lynn (1986), 'Petroleum and Political Pacts: the Transition to Democracy in Venezuela,' in Guillermo O'Donnell, Philipe Schmitter and Laurence Whitehead (eds), *Transitions from Authoritarian Rule: Latin America*, Baltimore, MD: Johns Hopkins University Press.

Karl, Terry Lynn (1990), 'Dilemmas or Democratization in Latin America,' *Comparative Politics*, 23(1), 1–21.

Kaufman, Robert (1986), 'Liberalization and Democratization in South America: Perspectives from the 1970s,' in Guillermo O'Donnell, Philipe Schmitter and Laurence Whitehead (eds), *Transitions from Authoritarian Rule: Comparative Perspectives*, Baltimore, MD: Johns Hopkins University Press.

Kaufman, Robert and Stallings, Barbara (eds) (1989), *Debt and Democracy in Latin America*, Boulder, CO: Westview Press.

Landau, Jacob, Oezbudun, Ergun, and Tachau, Frank (eds) (1980), *Electoral Politics in the Middle East*, New York: Croom Helm.

Lavy, Victor and Sheffer, Eliezer (1991), *Foreign Aid and Economic Development in the Middle East: Egypt, Syria, and Jordan*, New York: Praeger.

Lawless, Richard and Findlay, Anne (eds) (1984), *North Africa: Contemporary Politics and Economic Development*, New York: St Martin's Press.

Leveau, Rémy (1987), 'Stabilité du pouvoir monarchique et financement de la dette,' *Maghreb-Machrek*, 118 (October), 5–19.

Logfren, Hans (1993), 'Economic Policy in Egypt: a Breakdown in Reform Resistance?', *International Journal of Middle East Studies*, 25, 407–21.

Luciani, Giacomo (1987), 'Allocation vs. Production States: a Theoretical Framework,' in Hazem Beblawi and Giacomo Luciani (eds), *Nation, State and Integration in the Arab World*. Vol. 2: *The Rentier State*, London: Croom Helm.

Luciani, Giacomo (1988), 'Economic Foundations of Democracy and Authoritarianism: the Arab World in Comparative Perspective,' *Arab Studies Quarterly*, 10(4), 457–75.

Mahdavy, Hossain (1970), 'The Patterns and Problems of Economic Development in Rentier States: the Case of Iran,' in M.A. Cook (ed.), *Studies in the Economic History of the Middle East*, New York: Oxford University Press.

Mainwaring, Scott, O'Donnell, Guillermo and Valencuela, Samuel (eds) (1992), *Issues in Democratic Consolidation: The New South American Democracies in Comparative Perspective*, South Bend, IN: University of Notre Dame Press.

Malloy, James M. (ed.) (1997), *Authoritarianism and Corporatism in Latin America*, Pittsburgh, PA: University of Pittsburgh Press.

Mango, Andrew (1991), 'The Social Democratic Populist Party, 1983-1989,' in Metin Heper and Jacob Landau (eds), *Political Parties and Democracy in Turkey*, London: I.B. Tauris.

Marks, Jon (1993), 'Morocco: Assets to Sell,' *Middle East Economic Digest*, April 25, 7.

Middle East Research Institute of the University of Pennsylvania (1985a), *MERI Report: Egypt*, London: Croom Helm.

Middle East Research Institute of the University of Pennsylvania (1985b), *MERI Report: Kuwait*, London: Croom Helm.

Middle East Research Institute of the University of Pennsylvania (1985c), *MERI Report: Turkey*, London: Croom Helm.

The Middle East Review (various), London: Kogan Page.

Migdal, Joel (1987), 'Strong States, Weak States: Power and Accomodation,' in Myron Weiner and Samuel Huntington (eds), *Understanding Political Development*, Boston, MA: Little Brown, pp. 391-436.

Middle East Economic Digest (various).

Mitchell, Timothy (1999), 'Dreamland: the Neoliberalism of Your Desires,' *Middle East Report*, 29(1), 28-33.

Moench, Richard (1987), 'The May 1984 Elections in Egypt and the Question of Egypt's Stability,' in Linda Layne (ed.), *Elections in the Middle East: Implications of Recent Trends*, Boulder, CO: Westview Press.

Morrisson, Christian (1991), *Adjustment and Equity in Morocco*, Paris: Development Center, Organization for Economic Cooperation and Development.

El-Mossadeq, Rkia (1987), 'Morocco's International Economic Relations,' in I. William Zartman (ed.), *The Political Economy in Morocco*, New York: Praeger.

Munck, Gerardo (1994), 'Democratic Transitions in Comparative Perspective,' *Comparative Politics*, 26(3) (April), 355-75.

Munson, Henry Jr (1993), *Religion and Power in Morocco*, New Haven, CT: Yale University Press.

Nas, Tevfik F. and Odekon, Mehmet (eds) (1992), *Economics and Politics of Turkish Liberalization*, London: Associated University Presses.

Nelson, Harold D. (ed.) (1985), *Morocco: A Country Study*, 5th edn, Washington, DC: US Government Printing Office for Foreign Area Studies and the American University.

Nonneman, Gerd (1988), *Development, Aid and Administration in the Middle East*, New York: Routledge.

Nore, Peter and Turner, Terisa (eds) (1980), *Oil and Class Struggle*, London: Zed Press.

Norton, Augustus Richard (ed.) (1995, 1996), *Civil Society in the Middle East*, vols 1 and 2, New York: E.J. Brill.

O'Donnell, Guillermo (1979), *Modernization and Bureaucratic Authoritarianism*, Berkeley, CA: Institute of International Studies, University of California.

O'Donnell, Guillermo, Schmitter, Philippe and Whitehead, Laurence (eds) (1986), *Transitions from Authoritarian Rule: Comparative Perspectives*; *Transitions from Authoritarian Rule: Southern Europe*; *Transitions from Authoritarian Rule: Latin America*; *Transitions from Authoritarian Rule: Tentative Conclusions about Uncertain Democracies*; Baltimore, MD: Johns Hopkins University Press.

Ozbudun, Ergun (1990), 'Development of Democratic Government in Turkey,' in Larry Diamond et al. (eds), *Democracy in Developing Countries, Vol. 3. Asia*, Boulder, CO: Lynne Reinner.

Parker, Richard B (1984), *North Africa: Regional Tensions and Strategic Concerns*, New York: Praeger.

Peterson, James E (1988), *The Arab Gulf States: Steps toward Political Participation*, New York: Praeger.

Pfeifer, Karen (1999), 'How Tunisia, Morocco, Jordan and Even Egypt Became IMF Success Stories in the 1990s,' *Middle East Report*, 29(1), 23-7.

Pomfret, Richard (1987), 'Morocco's International Economic Relations,' in I. William Zartman (ed.), *The Political Economy of Morocco*, New York: Praeger.

Privatization International Ltd (1993), *Privatization Yearbook, 1993*, London: Privatization International.

Przeworski, Adam (1991), *Democracy and the Market: Political and Economic Reforms in Eastern Europe and Latin America*, Cambridge: Cambridge University Press.

Przeworski, Adam (1992), 'The Games of Transition,' in Scott Mainwaring et al. (eds), *Issues in Democratic Consolidation: The New South American Democracies in Comparative Perspective*, South Bend, IN: University of Notre Dame Press.

Remmer, Karen (1986), 'The Politics of Economic Stabilization: IMF Standby Programs in Latin America, 1954-84,' *Comparative Politics*, 19(1), 1-24.

Rhazaoui, Ahmed (1987), 'Recent Economic Trends: Managing the Indebtedness,' in I. William Zartman (ed.), *The Political Economy of Morocco*, New York: Praeger.

Richards, Alan and Waterbury, John (1990), *A Political Economy of the Middle East: State, Class and Economic Development*, Boulder, CO: Westview Press.

Rouquie, Alain (1986), 'Demilitarization and the Institutionalization of Military-dominated Politics in Latin America,' in G. O'Donnell (ed.),

Transitions from Authoritarian Rule: Comparative Perspectives, Baltimore, MD: Johns Hopkins University Press.

Sachs, Jeffrey (ed.) (1989), *Developing Country Debt and Economic Performance: The International Financial Sytem*, Chicago: University of Chicago Press.

Salame, Ghassan (ed.) (1995), *Democracy Without Democrats*, New York: St Martin's Press.

Sarah, Fayez (1990), *Political Parties and Political Power in Morocco*, London: Riyad El-Rayyes Books [in Arabic].

Satloff, Robert (1992), 'Jordan's Great Gamble: Economic Crisis and Political Reform,' in Henri J. Barkey (ed.), *The Politics of Economic Reform in the Middle East*, New York: St Martin's Press.

El-Sayyid, Mustapha (n.d.), 'The New Face of Authoritarianism in the Arab World,' unpublished paper.

Schmidt, William (1993), 'A Deluge of Foreign Assistance Fails to Revive Egypt's Stricken Economy,' *New York Times*, October 17, 10.

Schwedler, Jillian (ed.) (1996), *Toward a Civil Society in the Middle East*, Boulder, CO: Lynne Reinner.

Sehimi, Mustapha (1985), 'Les elections legislatives au Maroc,' *Maghreb-Machrek*, no. 107, pp. 23–51.

Sehimi, Mustapha (1986), *La Grande encyclopédie du Maroc: les institutions politiques*, Rabat: GEM.

Skocpol, Theda (1982), 'Rentier State and Shi'a Islam in the Iranian Revolution,' *Theory and Society*, 2(3), 265–304.

Sluglett, Peter and Farouk-Sluglett, Marion (1984), 'Modern Morocco: Political Immobilism, Economic Dependence,' in Richard Lawless and Allan Findlay (eds), *North Africa: Contemporary Politics and Economic Development*, New York: St Martin's Press, pp. 55–100.

Springborg, Robert (1989), *Mubarak's Egypt*, Boulder, CO: Westview Press.

Stallings, Barbara (1992), 'International Influence on Economic Policy: Debt, Stabilization, and Structural Reform,' in Stephan Haggard and Robert Kaufman (eds), *The Politics of Economic Adjustment*, Princeton, NJ: Princeton University Press.

Statistical Annex to the Annual Development Committee Report to Congress (1985-9), Washington, DC: US Government Printing Office.

Tachau, Frank (ed.) (1994), *Political Parties of the Middle East and North Africa*, Westport, CT: Greenwood Press.

Tessler, Mark (1982), 'Morocco: Institutional Pluralism and Monarchical Dominance,' in I. William Zartman et al. (eds), *Political Elites in Arab North Africa: Morocco, Algeria, Libya and Egypt*, New York: Longman.

Tessler, Mark (1987), 'Image and Reality in the Moroccan Political Economy,' in I. William Zartman (ed.), *The Political Economy of Morocco*, New York: Praeger.

Tessler, Mark and Entelis, John (1986), 'Kingdom of Morocco,' in David Long and Bernard Reich (eds), *The Government and Politics of the Middle East and North Africa*, 2nd edn, Boulder, CO: Westview Press.

Trimberger, Ellen Kay (1978), *Revolution from Above: Military Bureaucrats and Development in Japan, Turkey, Egypt and Peru*, New Brunswick, NJ: Transaction Books.

Tunay, Muharrem (1993), 'The New Turkish Right's Attempt at Hegemony,' in Atida Erlap, Muharrem Tunay and Birol Yesilada (eds), *The Political and Socioeconomic Transformation of Turkey*, Westport, CT: Praeger.

USAID/Egypt (1993), *Annual Report*, U.S. Agency for International Development in Cairo.

Vandewalle, Dirk (1992), 'Ben Ali's New Era: Pluralism and Economic Privatization in Tunisia,' in Henri J. Barkey (ed.), *The Politics of Economic Reform in the Middle East*, New York: St Martin's Press.

Al-Wafd (1984), January–June issues [in Arabic].

Waldner, David (1994), *The Formation of Precocious Keynesian States: Class Coalitions, State-building, and Economic Development in Syria and Turkey*, doctoral dissertation, University of California, Berkeley.

Waterbury, John (1983), *The Egypt of Nasser and Sadat: The Political Economy of Two Regimes*, Princeton, NJ: Princeton University Press.

Waterbury, John (1985), 'The "Soft State" and the Open Door: Egypt's Experience with Economic Liberalization, 1974–84,' *Comparative Politics*, 18(1), October, 65–83.

Waterbury, John (1992), 'Export-led Growth and the Center-right Coalition in Turkey,' in Tevfik Nas and Mehmet Odekon (eds), *Economics and Politics of Turkish Liberalization*, Bethlehem, PA: Lehigh University Press, pp. 44–72.

Weinbaum, Marvin (1986), *Egypt and the Politics of US Aid*, Boulder, CO: Westview Press.

World Bank (various), *World Bank Tables*, Washington, DC: World Bank.

World Bank (various), *World Development Reports*, Washington, DC: World Bank.

Zartman, I. William (ed.) (1987), *The Political Economy of Morocco*, New York: Praeger.

Zartman, I. William (1988), 'Opposition as Support of the State,' in Adeed Dawisha and I. William Zartman (eds), *Beyond Coercion: The Durability of the Arab State*, London: Croom Helm.

Zartman, I. William, et al. (1982), *Political Elites in Arab North Africa: Morocco, Algeria, Libya and Egypt*, New York: Longman.

Index